the Organised mum method

* and Organised dads!

Transform your home in 30 minutes a day

GEMMA BRAY

piatkus

PIATKUS

First published in Great Britain in 2019 by Piatkus

3 5 7 9 10 8 6 4

Copyright © Gemma Bray 2019

The moral right of the author has been asserted.

A CIP catalogue record for this book
is available from the British Library.

ISBN 978-0-349-42220-6

Typeset in Sabon by M Rules
Printed and bound in Great Britain by
Clays Ltd, Elcograf S.p.A.

Papers used by Piatkus are from well-managed forests
and other responsible sources.

Piatkus
An imprint of
Little, Brown Book Group
Carmelite House
50 Victoria Embankment
London EC4Y 0DZ

An Hachette UK Company
www.hachette.co.uk

www.improvementzone.co.uk

This book is dedicated to everyone in TeamTOMM.
Thank you for putting your faith in me.

Contents

Part 3: Troubleshooting – How to Stay On Track

Part 4: You Can't Clean on an Empty Stomach

Part 5: Christmas – Be Prepared!

Acknowledgements

I have loved every second of writing this book (even the edits!). Thank you to everyone who has helped to make my dream of a book a reality. I still have to pinch myself sometimes.

Thank you to Chippy for believing in me (and also for putting up with my '*I have an idea!*' WhatsApp messages in the middle of the night). You have become a true friend. Thank you to Taressa for being so generous and joining the gang to help me to understand the new world I seem to have found myself in. To my team of moderators who run the Facebook group: Adele, Amy, Chippy, Fi, Gemma, Janell, Jenny, Jill, Lottie, Louisa, Sarah and Vicki. You guys are seriously *amazing*. I couldn't do it without you. Thank you soooooooooo much. Thank you to Zoe, Clara, Jillian and all of the publishing team at Piatkus and Little, Brown. Thank you for being gentle with me as I negotiated the book-writing process for the first time.

To my mum, dad and big sister, thank you for being my cheerleaders, it truly means the world to have such a close family. Big *big* love. Thank you to my amazing children Tom,

Jonny and Ben for inspiring me to start TOMM in the first place. (Oh and thank you for being such enthusiastic recipe testers. Even on that week when we had the same meal five nights running!)

And finally to Mike, thank you for holding my hand throughout. I hope you will hold my hand forever.

Introduction

I wasn't always organised. I wasn't the girl at school who had an enviable selection of highlighter pens or immaculately covered books. Nor was I neat and tidy like I am now. I had to learn. In fact, even my own mum finds it hilarious that I am writing a book about cleaning and organisation. But I am a very different woman from the teenager who once found a week-old packed lunch under her bed. (I'm getting that story out now so that my mum can't share her favourite anecdote from my childhood with you once this book is published.) To be fair, though, my mum did once offer to teach me to iron. My response? 'When I'm rich and famous I will have an entourage to do that kind of stuff for me!' Oh, the naivety of youth. I still don't iron much, however, because I've found loads of ways to cut the ironing pile down to almost zero – but more on that a little later on.

When I was younger, running an organised home held no value for me – that was until I had children. It was my catalyst for change, and, believe me, if I can change, so can you. In my early twenties I found myself married and pregnant. I realised (quickly) that kids pretty much change everything. I suddenly became overwhelmed by the number of things I should be doing in the house. I was a mum, and in my head that meant I had to have an immaculate home, with banana bread baking in the oven, fresh flowers on the kitchen table and Cath Kidston everything. I couldn't afford Cath Kidston, so that meant I was already on the back foot.

As much as my mum tried to teach me to iron, I really didn't know the basics of what I needed to be doing with the housework and how often I needed to be doing it. How often did I need to clean the loo? How regularly do the bed sheets need changing? What are all these strange accessories that come with the vacuum cleaner?

It really overwhelmed me, and I started to drive myself into the ground with the amount of stuff I was trying to achieve in an attempt to keep up with the perfect-mum ideal that I had created in my mind. I distinctly remember the health visitor coming to the house when my eldest was just days old and I was still healing from the birth. I thought that if my bathroom wasn't super-clean she would think that I was a bad mum. I got down on my hands and knees and scrubbed the floor until you could eat your dinner off it. (Not something you would want to be doing when you are recovering from a forceps delivery.) Nevertheless, I did it, because I thought that was what was expected of me. And the irony of this story is that she never even asked to use the bathroom.

It soon became clear that I needed to approach life differently. I was over-cleaning and exhausted. I felt as though I was on a treadmill of never-ending chores, and I never really had time to do anything fun. I hardly saw my friends, and my life was a cycle of cleaning, baby care and sleeping.

I was also a bit of a rubbish cook. I grew up in the 1980s when turkey drummers and Pop-Tarts were king. My mum and dad owned a fish and chip shop in Manchester and used to work 12-hour days, six days a week. They didn't have the time or the energy to start cooking again when we got home, so it was quick, easy food.

When I had my first baby, I was running a fish and chip shop of my very own, and my diet was still 'something' with chips and beans most nights. I quickly realised that in a few months I would be cooking for a newly weaning baby and oven chips were not going to make the grade. This meant that cooking was something else that I needed to add to the list of things I had to learn. I didn't want to eat beige food any more, nor did I want my life to revolve around housework. Before I became a mum I was sold this amazing vision of motherhood, but of course life isn't the way it is depicted in magazines, on Instagram or in the ads you see on TV of mums dressed in white skinny jeans feeding their baby carrot purée (never a practical combination).

I needed a cunning plan. Not one to be beaten, I sat down at my kitchen table (where there were still no fresh flowers) and wrote a housekeeping plan on a piece of notepaper, then I stuck it on the fridge. The Organised Mum Method was born or, as everyone who follows the plan calls it, TOMM. It was easy to follow, it worked, and it got everything done in 30 minutes a day from Monday to Friday (I didn't want to spend my weekends cleaning and doing the laundry). Little did I realise that this plan would become a way of life for me, and that over a decade later it would have evolved into a blog that would revolutionise the way other people view housework.

I also taught myself how to cook. After a little practice, I realised that I actually enjoyed cooking, but now that I had a new baby on my hip I didn't have the time to spend hours chopping and stirring. I began to teach myself simple recipes that were easy to make and tasted delicious, and I added to them and perfected them as the years went by. I have included some of these recipes in this book. They are perfect for people who don't have much time but who love good food. They won't have you chained to the hob in the early evening – which, as any parent knows, is the time of day that is already fraught, without throwing cooking into the mix.

That was 12 years ago. Fast-forward to today and I have three children (all boys), a dog (also a boy) and a husband (a man). I have followed TOMM the whole time, no matter what was going on in my life. It has seen me through a divorce and becoming a single mum to two young children, running a business (two fish and chip shops – I make the *best* mushy peas), teaching antenatal classes and being on 24-hour call as a doula. TOMM has remained consistent throughout those various stages of my life. Not only was it essential when I was a single mum but now that I am happily married to Mike, it provides us with a way of managing the housework equally while we both work full-time.

I promise you that TOMM works. Not only that: it is life changing.

If you want the same things as I did 12 years ago, let me

hold your hand, stroke your hair and guide you through the chaos to a calmer and happier home. We'll have some laughs on the way, and hopefully you'll see that the housework doesn't need to be overwhelming or time-consuming. I will show you how to fit the housework into your busy life, whether you live alone, work shifts, have a large family or have just moved out of home for the first time. Together we'll tackle some of the most common cleaning conundrums, such as how to minimise (or avoid) the ironing and how to make sure your odd socks don't breed.

This book isn't just for mums; we all know that being female doesn't mean that you are the default housekeeper. This book is for families, couples, shift workers, grandparents and everyone in between. You might even like to buy a copy for your grown-up kids who are just about to start university in the hope that they won't have to bring home bags of laundry every time they visit.

I aim to make housework as easy and as painless as possible, but I am a realistic woman (that is the Northerner in me): I know that there will be times when you might not feel like cleaning, cooking or doing anything other than sitting on the sofa and eating your way through a whole tube of Pringles. But these are the times when I will have you covered: I have paved the way and found the shortcuts – and in this book I will pass them on to you.

Are you ready to start your journey? Let's go!

PART 1

Getting Started

1

The Organised Mum Method (TOMM) and Why it Works

'There's more to life than housework.' This little saying is so true, but I suspect you weren't expecting to read it in a book that is dedicated to it. I strongly believe that we need to learn to balance the need for housework with actually living. We can't abandon the dusting completely, but neither should we let it rule us.

When I first shared TOMM with the great British public I never in my wildest dreams thought that it would become the phenomenon that it has. I followed TOMM privately for years before I shared it, and for that reason I hold it very close to my heart. It gave me a way of keeping everything together as a mum, enabled me to work and to spend time with my friends and family, all without sacrificing my sanity and without the house falling apart at the seams. It was only two years ago, on New Year's Eve, that I decided to go public with TOMM, and it was all down to Tom, my first born – although it is a total coincidence with the name. He dared me to share my way of cleaning with the world. At first I was nervous; at the time Instagram was full of beautiful celebs showing off their arty avocado-on-toast shots. But it seems that people needed TOMM in their life as much as I did.

The first year was a whirlwind: I went from being a mum of three children (still on maternity leave with my youngest) to a blogger, YouTuber and Instagrammer. For someone who is not very tech-savvy it was a very steep learning curve. But one of the most heartwarming things for me is that even though the rise of TOMM's popularity was fast, so many of you who followed me at the very start are still following along today. In fact, I scrolled all the way back to my first Instagram post a few days ago, and one of the people who liked it is now one of the moderators for our Facebook group – how amazing is that?

We have built up an incredible TeamTOMM community, and now you are part of that, too. It is so lovely to have you with us. Here we are, two years later, and the nation has taken TOMM to its heart – it has even flown as far afield as the United States, Australia and New Zealand. This always makes me smile, because something that I thought up one day at my kitchen table has started to transform the lives of so many. Every day I get messages from people who have turned to TOMM and found that it has revolutionised the way they look at housework. It is helping people's mental health and giving them much more time to focus on their families, careers and hobbies. What's not to love?

I've even been stopped in the cleaning aisle of the supermarket and been asked my opinion on which is the best product to remove limescale from a shower door. I love this so much – so if you ever see me out and about, give me a wave. I still live and breathe the method. And that's simply because it works. It enables me to do my job, have time where I can sit down and play with my kids and gives me housework-free weekends.

WHY TOMM WORKS

TOMM is a simple, efficient housekeeping plan that makes it easy to keep on top of everything in your home and leaves you free to do all the things you'd rather be doing. My motto:

GET IN, GET IT DONE AND THEN GET OUTTA THERE!

The method requires just 30 minutes of cleaning each day, Monday to Friday. Weekends are purposefully kept housework-free so that you can enjoy your time off without having to do a mammoth clean. Each day, from Monday to Thursday, has its own focus room (living room on Monday, bedrooms on Tuesday, and so on) and these never change. Every Friday a room gets an additional deep clean – called the Friday Focus – rotating on an eight-week cycle.

TOMM is really easy to follow once you get started, but that can often be the hardest part. Before I go into more detail about the method, let's consider what makes TOMM so special and how TOMM can work for you and your individual circumstances. (Go straight to Chapter 3 if you're already familiar with the method and you are just looking for a refresher.)

THE SUPER-EFFICIENT 30 MINUTES

I know just how easy it can be to let housework creep into every part of your day. You start dusting, and then a few minutes later (bored) you pick up your phone, have a little bit of a scroll through Facebook or Instagram, and, before you know it, 20 minutes have passed and you're still holding your duster but no dusting has actually taken place. Sound familiar?

This is why it seems that housework takes forever. If you are not focusing on the task at hand and are allowing yourself to become distracted, it will (obviously) take longer. And let's get real, sometimes anything can seem more appealing than a job that you don't want to do. How many times have you become faux busy in order to avoid a task that you've been putting off? We allow ourselves to get distracted, but all we are doing is putting off the inevitable. It's far better to get your head down, focus, get it done and then get outta there!

This is why TOMM works in 30-minute chunks – to give you a solid 30 minutes of distraction-free time. If you have never done anything like this before, I promise you that you will be shocked at how much you can achieve. What's more, 30 minutes isn't that long, so it can be shoehorned into your day. I usually do mine first thing in the morning. I like to leave the house knowing that when I get in after a long day I won't have to lift a finger.

If you are a bit sceptical and fancy a bit of a challenge, try this: put down this book, set your timer for 30 minutes, and use that time to tackle a job that you have been putting off. I guarantee that once the 30 minutes is up you'll feel fab about the fact that you've ticked a job off your list – you might even be motivated to tackle something else.

The amount of cleaning you can get done in 30 minutes is always quite staggering too. You will be shocked at how much is achievable. Again, if you are thinking *This woman is crazy!* set your timer for 15 minutes and see how much you can smash through. And that is just in 15 minutes – imagine what you could achieve in 30! I get so many messages from people saying that they are bowled over by how much they got done in the time. It isn't just me who is operating on some kind of turbo-charged cleaning speed.

The 30 minutes, however, is only half of the story.

THE FRIDAY FOCUS

The real key to TOMM, and the reason why your home will get cleaner and cleaner every week you follow the method, is the Friday Focus. Let me explain how it works. Your TOMM week is structured so that every Monday to Thursday you will have the same jobs to do. These never change. After a few weeks you will know them off by heart and you will be into your stride – you won't even have to check what you are supposed to be doing. But every Friday we ratchet it up, and an area of your home will get a deeper level of focus, a mini spring clean, if you like. By the way, if you follow TOMM, you won't have to spring clean again because your home will always have a good rotational cleaning system going on. That's another added bonus of the method.

The Friday Focus operates over an eight-week cycle, so every week you will be in a new area of the home, going one level deeper than you usually clean during Monday to Thursday.

I told you it was simple. TOMM will give you structure. You won't suddenly find yourself with a few spare minutes and panic about how you can use them to your best advantage. You now have a list and a system and you will tick everything off as you go along.

DON'T AIM FOR PERFECTION

A little word on realism and cleaning your home while bearing in mind that people have to live there:

TOMM is a realistic method for the real world. Pinterest-perfect homes rarely exist, and believe me when I say that trying to achieve one will break you. I know, because I tried.

When I decided to talk about TOMM online, I started by dipping my toe into the water of Instagram. It felt like I was whispering about my method in a massive room filled with people who were posting pictures of gorgeous kitchens and living rooms – homes that looked like they would have been perfectly suited to an episode of *Grand Designs*. This made me feel uncomfortable for two reasons:

1   I don't think that showing people an unobtainable lifestyle is motivational. It is totally unrealistic for many of us to live some of the lifestyles that we are shown on social media, and the aspirations that are born from scrolling can be damaging to our mental health.

2   I know for a fact that in some of the pictures you see of perfectly straightened coffee tables there is a whole heap of mess shoved just out of shot. Just as people might Photoshop their bodies when they post that bikini picture, be wary of the perfect-home pictures too.

Our homes need to function. Our home houses our family – that means lots of bodies breathing, eating, sleeping and just generally getting on with life. If you try to maintain a perfect show home, you will always be straightening the coffee table and forever cleaning up. Is this what you really want to be doing with your life?

This is how I look at it; I am never going to look like Cindy Crawford (circa that Pepsi advert). No matter how hard I try, my hair will never do that and I won't ever be able to wear a cream body suit with denim hot pants (because of kids, Pringles and wine). Similarly, my house is never going to look like one of those gorgeous beach houses in the Hamptons, all white linen, white roses and perfectly minimalist (because of kids, Pringles and wine).

Let go of perfect. Trust in TOMM and give yourself permission to stop after the 30 minutes are up. If you follow

TOMM, you will be doing enough cleaning, and your mental health will thank you for it.

GEM'S TOP TIP

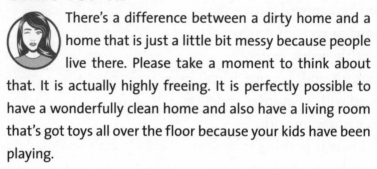

There's a difference between a dirty home and a home that is just a little bit messy because people live there. Please take a moment to think about that. It is actually highly freeing. It is perfectly possible to have a wonderfully clean home and also have a living room that's got toys all over the floor because your kids have been playing.

WHICH TYPE OF CLEANER ARE YOU?

By now, I will hopefully have convinced you that TOMM is the way forward. And you will be ready to join thousands of others all over the world who are part of TeamTOMM. But first we need to look at how you are already cleaning. You are reading this book because you want to change how you run your home, and I can't help you change until you understand what your stumbling block is and how TOMM can help you. Once you have worked out where you are going wrong, you will be able to get yourself back on track and start cleaning smarter, not harder. So let's get down to it: which type of cleaner are you?

The weekender

If you are one of those people who spends their whole Saturday desperately trying catch up on the housework that you have missed during the week, this book is for you. If you want to reclaim your weekends and spread the housework over the week (without actually realising you are doing it), stick around, because it will blow your mind when you are faced with a Saturday and Sunday that are yours to do whatever you want with.

There is nothing more demoralising than spending hours upon hours cleaning only for it to be undone in 30 minutes. And this is what happens if you are currently doing a mammoth clean once a week. Your home will look great when you eventually collapse with a cup of tea (or wine) and exhaustedly survey all your hard work. But hark, what is that we hear yonder? That, my friends, is the sound of your toddler thundering into the room to undo all your graft.

When you clean the TOMM way, you not only get your weekends back, but you also spread the cleaning over the week so that the house is always in a fit state for visitors and the dirt never gets out of hand. You won't be running around in a panic trying to speed-clean the house when the mother-in-law springs a surprise visit on you. For those of you who are currently stuck in this mode, please don't worry, because I have a strategy coming up in Chapter 11 for when situations like this occur, because they will occur, it is just part of life.

The ostrich

If you have buried your head in the sand for a bit too long and your home resembles Primark in the sales, don't worry. Give me a week and I can help you tame the mess.

First step – do not panic. Your home didn't get this way overnight, so it is unrealistic to think that you can get it back to its best in a weekend. Don't fall into the trap of jumping up and shouting 'Right, that's it, I'm going to declutter every single cupboard, cull the garage, the shed and the loft and we're going to get organised today!'

The easy part is pulling everything out of cupboards, but then you get that sinking feeling when it dawns on you that the hard bit is next. Because now you have to clean and organise and do runs to the charity shop and list things on eBay, which all takes time and energy, which might be in short supply given everything else that you need to be doing. By this point the tiredness sets in and you might be tempted to move out, or just shut the door. You're back to head-in-the-sand mode.

We're not going to do that. We are going to tackle one space at a time and you are going to use the Messy House Boot Camp to finally get control once and for all. After you have completed the Boot Camp you will be ready to start TOMM proper and join the 30 minutes-a-day crew.

(A little word about the Boot Camp: halfway through the Boot Camp you might hate me a little tiny bit, but I promise that once you are done you will love me again. I just have to give you a bit of tough love to push you towards your goals.)

The firefighter

If you belong to the firefighter camp, you might be reading this in such a heightened state of frazzled exhaustion that it's possible that not everything I will say will be going in. If you feel that you are constantly picking up after the kids/ your partner/the dog, you are probably just chasing your tail and not actually achieving anything. People most likely to be in this camp are new parents, the parents of a toddler and working parents – so that's basically all parents then.

I am going to need you to focus. Sit down, make yourself a cup of tea, and read the following statement over and over until it has sunk in: I am getting nowhere cleaning like this. It feels as if I am taking two steps forward and one step backward. I am achieving nothing. I need to change my strategy before I burn out.

This is where TOMM will help you. There is no doubt about it: the firefighters among us need structure in order to regain control over the housework. And my method gives you that structure. When you come down in the morning, you will know what you are meant to be doing, and pretty soon you will be a well-oiled cleaning machine and your home will be an oasis of calm.

I totally get it. I have three kids, so I know the chaos that can be caused in one room while you are toiling away in another. You have just spent an hour cleaning the lounge, and to your horror realise that in that time the rest of the house has been trashed while your kids have been left unattended.

The good news is that not only am I going to help you get the kids and everyone else you live with on-board, but I'm also going to help you put the correct strategies in place to ensure that you won't be chasing your tail or drowning in laundry.

The perfectionist

TOMM isn't just for people who have lost control of the housework, it has also helped thousands who feel as though the housework has taken control of *them*. This was, of course, me back when I was cleaning the bathroom floor just before the health visitor popped round. My cleaning was taking over my days, and it was making me miserable.

Obsessive cleaning can take over people's lives, and I have spoken to many TOMMers who have successfully used the method to help take back control. Putting a time limit on the housework puts a full stop on the cleaning day and eliminates the guilt creeping in that you haven't done enough. What's more, having a clear structure means that everything gets covered and you won't waste time repeating the same jobs unnecessarily.

I don't want you to waste your life cleaning for hours on end just to get demoralised when the kids storm in after footy and leave their sweaty kit all over the bedroom floor.

TOMM is going to help you address the balance and get your life back.

Let's get started.

2

Where Do You Start?

Are we all assembled and raring to go? It would be madness if I expected you all to be able to start at the same point. Some of you will be joining TeamTOMM from a standing start and will be able to crack on with the 30 minutes a day right away, but others might have to play a little bit of catch-up.

Perhaps you have had a cleaner up until now, but you have just started maternity leave and this means that your budget is stretched and a cleaner is now a luxury that you can no longer afford. If this (or something similar) is your current situation, your home will no doubt be looking pretty decent and you just need a system to help keep it that way. Or perhaps you have just moved into your very first home and you are looking for a way to keep it looking (and smelling) brand new.

On the other hand, there will be those of you who will need a little leg-up to get to the point where you are able to maintain your home in just 30 minutes a day. Perhaps you have just had a baby and, up until now, your home was easily tamed, but since your little bundle of joy arrived, things have become a little more challenging. That's fine. Everyone has different starting points. Wherever you are in your housekeeping journey I don't want you to worry, we'll all be at the same place soon. It will just take some of you a little longer to get there. Think of it as taking the scenic route and me as your effervescent tour guide making it as fun as possible along the way.

WHAT STAGE ARE YOU AT RIGHT NOW?

We have reached the point where some of you will stick around with me here, whereas others will be able to move forward a little bit quicker.

If you feel as though your house has been neglected for whatever reason recently (perhaps you have been ill, work has taken over or . . . well, kids), then you need to stick with this section. But if you feel as though your home has been kept clean and tidy, but you are looking for a little structure to your housework and/or you need help in reining in excessive cleaning, then move straight on to the section on page 36 called Let's Get this Party Started! Of course, you are free to come back to this section at any time; just look upon it as your housekeeping reset button.

I want you to think of this book as your whip and with it you are going to whip your home back into shape. Show no mercy.

YOU CAN'T CLEAN CLUTTER

Have you seen that episode of *Friends* where Rachel tries to clean up for Monica but all that happens is she just dusts *under* piles of paperwork and magazines? Oh, how the audience laughs. The joke was on Rachel, because in order for her to truly clean up she needed to tidy all the mess away first. But she didn't, so the room didn't look any different. Don't be Rachel. And, while we are on the subject don't be Monica – we are aiming for somewhere in between.

Sometimes you can't see the wood for the trees (or the dining table for the piles of washing). If you are going to embark on TOMM, you need to give yourself a head start. There is no point in setting aside 30 minutes to clean if all you do is move piles of clutter from one side of the room to the other.

Let's do a very quick home audit – so that you can base your next move on what you see in front of you. Take a look around your home and ask yourself the following:

1 Do you see piles of clutter and a messy house?

Or

2 Do you see a fairly clutter-free home that needs a good spruce-up?

If you answered 1, you need to tackle the Clutter Buster first and then move on to the Messy House Boot Camp.

If you answered 2, you can go straight to Attacking a Messy House and the Messy House Boot Camp (see pages 31–36).

TACKLING THE CLUTTER

How many out-of-date Next catalogues do you have? Do you have a room in your home that is just a storage room? Are you storing stuff that you no longer use? Do you crave more storage, and are you running out of space? If this sounds familiar and you're nodding your head, don't even think about cleaning anything until you have sifted through the mountains of champagne corks from first dates, shells from summer holidays and clothes that no longer fit. You definitely need to embrace the Clutter Buster.

I know that you are starting on the back foot here, and it seems like you have been kept behind a year at school, but if you jumped in with your 30 minutes a day now, you would become despondent fast and you would then abandon TOMM altogether, and that wouldn't be a good thing. Your home hasn't got this way overnight, so you need to be patient with yourself and trust the process. Give yourself permission to take the time you need to get the job done properly. Think of it like this: you are building the foundations for a long-term housekeeping method that will save you time (and probably a whole lot of heartache) in the coming years, so you need to make sure that those foundations are strong. Your home and your mind will thank you for it. Living in a cluttered environment can be stressful, and when you can't see your hob for the amount of stuff that's piled on top of it, it can make even the easiest of tasks (like boiling an egg) hard work.

The Clutter Buster is less about cleaning and much more about getting rid of excess stuff. No one needs five winter coats (especially if you don't have the wardrobe space) and if you clear the clutter before moving on to the Boot Camp, you'll be raring to go and smashing through your 30 minutes on TOMM like a rock star.

GEM'S TOP TIP

This is my decluttering golden rule – know your exits! Before you start decluttering you must have a plan in place for all the stuff you are about to get rid of. Have an exit route in mind, whether that be a skip or a way of taking it all to the recycling centre or charity shop. If you don't do this you run the risk of bagging it all up for it to never actually leave the house, which means that in reality all you will have done is move it from one place in your home to another.

THE CLUTTER BUSTER

(No timer needed for this.)

The amount of time that this is going to take will depend on these things:

1. The size of your home.
2. The amount of rooms that need your help.
3. The amount of time you have free.
4. The amount of clutter you have.

If you are lacking in motivation, head over to the Facebook group (search TeamTOMM on Facebook) and we can collectively keep you motivated/kick your butt (whichever you prefer).

Before you start

- **Be realistic** You can only keep the amount of stuff you are able to store, so unless you are willing to pay for storage, you are going to have to prepare yourself for some serious culling.
- **Plan the exit route** Before you start filling your bin bags, think about what you are going to do with the stuff. You don't want to end up in a situation where you have piles of rubbish sitting outside in the back garden with no way to get it shifted.

- **Don't start what you can't finish** Make sure you have enough time to complete the tasks you have chosen to do, or you will become demotivated and despondent.

3, 2, 1 – go!

Pick a room

(only do one room at a time)

Sort the clutter into 3 piles:
1 Bin it
2 Keep it
3 Donate it

Take before-and-after pictures to keep you motivated.
Keep going! ←

Start in the left-hand corner of your room and work your way around clockwise. Have a one-touch policy: if you pick it up, sort it into a pile.

Top tips

- Most councils have a disposal service for bulky items such as fridges and sofas.
- If you are up to your neck in rubbish, it might be worth hiring a skip.
- If you are overly sentimental and are still clinging on to the champagne cork from New Year's Eve 1996, you might need to reassess your emotional connection to inanimate objects.
- A word about clothes: if it no longer fits, or if you haven't worn it for 12 months, let it go.

Knowing where to start decluttering can be tricky. It can be overwhelming looking at a sea of mess. But start we must and a great place to take the plunge is your wardrobe.

My decluttering tips for your wardrobe

Most of us have far too many clothes. Not only do they take up valuable space but if you find yourself staring blankly at your crammed clothes rails every morning, hoping for inspiration, then it wastes valuable time too. Here's how to slay the formidable beast that is the wardrobe that won't close:

1 **At the turn of the season** pack away anything that you won't be wearing. Pack away thick winter coats and jumpers or flimsy summer dresses and shorts. Pack them away neatly folded and put them somewhere safe. This does two things: (1) it keeps your wardrobe as clutter-free as possible; and, as an added bonus (2) it is like Christmas when you unpack your old clothes again. I always find something I forgot I had. It is like going shopping without spending any money. Have you ever heard of that phrase 'shop your wardrobe'? Well, this is just like that.

2 **When you pack away your clothes,** be realistic. If there is anything that you haven't worn, that no longer fits or has seen better days, now is the time for you to say goodbye. There is a nifty little trick to help you do this. Tie something around your hangers (such as a

piece of string or ribbon) and when you wear the item of clothing, take the ribbon/string off. This way, when it comes to the next wardrobe sort-out you will clearly see the clothing that you haven't worn, and it will mean that most of the hard work will already be done for you when the time comes to have another seasonal edit.

3 **Only buy clothes that fit** This might sound very obvious. But I know that there will be some of you (I have been very guilty of this in the past) who will promise yourselves that you will squeeze into a pair of slightly too small jeans when you buy them. But let's be truthful: it won't happen. What will more than likely happen, however, is that the jeans will just sit in your wardrobe and remind you of a fad diet. I had an amazing dress once (that was a liiiittle bit too tight) and I swear I could hear it laughing at me every time I opened my wardrobe. We don't need that type of negativity in our lives. Get rid of it!

4 **Buy clothes that suit your lifestyle** Do not buy clothes that fit in with your dream lifestyle. I am a mum of three boys, and I work from home. Therefore, what need do I have for a smart work outfit? I can't remember the last time I even went into an office. Shoes with heels? Forget it. I do stare wistfully sometimes at the lovely fashion bloggers in their immaculate dry-clean-only dresses, but it is not for me (I'm too prone to spilling my lunch); anything I buy like that (although it might be beautiful) won't get worn. I don't go there any more.

5 **And finally, if you hate ironing** as much as I do, don't buy clothes that need tons of ironing, because you will wear them once, wash them and then realise you have to plug the iron in, and they will languish all sad and crumpled in your wardrobe until the end of time (or your next wardrobe declutter). I will talk you through how to keep you ironing pile as small as possible a little later on, so make sure you stick around.

Be realistic with your time

Once you've tackled your wardrobe, it's time to broaden your horizons. This is where you can benefit from thousands of TOMMers who have pioneered this path for you. Hear me when I say this. Do not fall into the age-old trap of going in like a bull in a china shop and pulling every item you own out of every drawer and cupboard in the house. Your home will end up looking like you've thrown everything up in the air and left stuff where it landed, and you will end up crying in the corner wishing you hadn't started. You will lose your energy and motivation approximately halfway through. This is usually at the exact point of no return, where you have emptied all the cupboards and you have to put everything back. It really is soul-destroying. I get so many pictures sent to me from TOMMers who have fallen into this trap and are wailing at the task that now confronts them. Set your sights on a small area: attack that bit, then move on.

Operate a 'one in, one out' approach

Once you have decluttered your home and you are happy with how it looks, you will need to have a strategy under your belt that means it stays this way. Of course, you will be following TOMM, but this won't stop you from bringing in rogue items that over time will start to build up that clutter mountain again. For those of us with kids, Happy Meal toys and party bag tat are the worst culprits. Let me suggest a really easy way to stop this from happening:

If you buy a new coat, make sure you get rid of an old coat. **If you buy your child a new toy,** remove another toy from your home. This way you will have the same amount of stuff and the status quo will be maintained.

ATTACKING A MESSY HOUSE

I'm going to give you a word of warning: this isn't going to be an easy week. You might look at the list below and recoil in horror. But remember the TOMM golden rule: your home didn't get this way overnight, so it stands to reason that it won't suddenly turn into an immaculate gleaming palace immediately. This is housework, not magic. In order for your home to be transformed, hard graft needs to take place.

Look at the Messy House Boot Camp as your rite of passage to the 30 minutes a day. The 30 minutes will seem like a breeze once you get there, but you have to put some work in to achieve your housework nirvana. The amount of work you have to put in, of course, depends on the state of your home. Only you will know what needs to be done. Whether or not you need to put on a hazmat suit is down to you and your individual home.

The main difference between the Messy House Boot Camp and TOMM is that there is no timer for the Boot Camp. You basically have to suck it up until you are done. I know this sounds harsh, and I know that come Wednesday you will probably be cursing me, but by the end of it you will love me again. And to be honest, I am quite willing to take the hit if it means that you have a clean and sparkling house that you will be easily able to keep on top of. Tough love is in operation here.

Of course, you don't have to tackle this alone. If you have a partner and/or kids, for example, I am willing to bet that it isn't just your mess that needs sorting through. It will get done much quicker if you divide the load and everyone does their bit. It can even be cathartic. While you are occupied doing simple things, like sorting through piles of paperwork, quite often meaningful chats spontaneously happen. Decluttering is a journey and, as with many journeys, it is much more enjoyable when shared.

If one week is not enough

A quick word to the overwhelmed: if you feel that you won't be able to achieve the Boot Camp in one week, this doesn't have to be a hard-and-fast rule. Spread it out over two weeks or more, if you need to. Just remember to maintain momentum. And don't panic about bedrooms. If you have kids and need to tackle their rooms then you can either get them involved – as I suggested above – or, if they are too young to pitch in, then you might need to spread tackling the bedrooms over a couple of days. Remember, this is not a test of speed or endurance, there is no medal for the quickest completed Boot Camp. Take it at a pace that is right for you and if that means dividing the bedrooms over a couple of days then so be it.

If you work long hours and can't commit the time it will take to carry out the Boot Camp in the timetable suggested, you are the perfect candidate to spread it out over a couple of weekends. There are no hard and fast rules. I won't be in your home, standing over you with a stop watch and clipboard. Make it work for you.

If you have extra rooms that aren't included in the Boot Camp – for example, a play room, dining room or study – my advice is to have a look at your home as a whole and work out if there are any areas where additional rooms can be tagged on. Can the dining room be included with the kitchen or the play room added to the living room day?

OK, enough of the talk, it's time for some action. Rubber gloves at the ready.

THE MESSY HOUSE BOOT CAMP

Monday: living room

- ✓ Declutter
- ✓ Clean the windows and mirrors
- ✓ Wash throws and pet bedding
- ✓ Dust everything
- ✓ Clean the skirting boards
- ✓ Vacuum under the sofa cushions
- ✓ Vacuum under the furniture
- ✓ Mop if applicable

Tuesday: bedrooms

- ✓ Declutter
- ✓ Have a beauty product/ toy cull
- ✓ Clean the windows and mirrors
- ✓ Vacuum and flip the mattresses
- ✓ Dust everything
- ✓ Clean the skirting boards
- ✓ Vacuum
- ✓ Change the bedding

Wednesday: entrance hall and stairs

- ✓ Declutter
- ✓ Have a coat and shoes cull
- ✓ Clean the windows and mirrors
- ✓ Dust everything
- ✓ Clean the banisters and skirting boards
- ✓ Vacuum under the furniture

Thursday: kitchen

- ✓ Empty the crumbs from the toaster
- ✓ Clean out the cutlery drawer(s)
- ✓ Clean out the fridge
- ✓ Dust the blinds
- ✓ Clean the windows
- ✓ Clean the microwave
- ✓ Clean down the tiles
- ✓ Clean the oven and hob
- ✓ Clean all the worktops
- ✓ Clean the cupboard fronts
- ✓ Clean the kickboards
- ✓ Vacuum and mop

Friday: bathrooms

- ✓ Dust the extractor fan
- ✓ Clean out the cabinets
- ✓ Clean the shower curtain/give the shower screen a good scrub
- ✓ Clean the wall tiles
- ✓ Clean the windows and mirrors
- ✓ Scrub the toilet, shower, bath and sink
- ✓ Clean the floor, paying particular attention to the floor around the loo
- ✓ Wash the bathmat

When you've completed the Messy House Boot Camp or the Clutter Buster, make sure you give yourself the praise you deserve. I know it's hard when you are starting from scratch, and it can be extremely overwhelming to realise how much the housework has built up. But once you are done you will find it all so much easier to keep on top of everything, and following TOMM will seem like a walk in the park.

LET'S GET THIS PARTY STARTED!

You've now cleared the decks. Well done! Now that you have completed the Clutter Buster and Boot Camp challenges you are ready to start the regular 30-minutes-a-day method and get cracking with the nitty-gritty of maintaining your home.

Before we all start cleaning and polishing like mad, there is a point that I think needs to be made. Housework doesn't have to be complicated, and even though I seem to have written a whole book on it, it can actually be very simple. Very often as humans we are guilty of over-egging the pudding, and by this I mean that sometimes we make life far too complicated for ourselves. That is why TOMM is such a great concept, it is simple and effective, and, more importantly, it works.

The one thing that I want you to do now is to trust me and to trust in TOMM. For those of you who identified yourself as perfectionists in the previous chapter, it is going to take a mind-set shift for you to clean only one room a day and to also put a time limit on how long you clean for. But I want to reassure you that you only need to do your 30 minutes. I promise you that if you are working efficiently (procrastinators, I am looking at you), you will be doing enough cleaning. I really don't want to see people toiling away any more than they have to.

In this section I am going to hold your hand and walk you through how to maintain your little corner of the planet in just 30 minutes a day. I am going to give you a manageable system that will take all the guesswork and stress out of the housekeeping. You will no longer dread a surprise guest turning up and, more importantly, you will have more time for yourself so that you can do the fun stuff that you love.

THE ORGANISED MUM METHOD EXPLAINED

I've already outlined how TOMM came to be born, along with the basics of the method and it's no-nonsense approach to housework but let's look at it in more detail. TOMM operates on a three-level system and each of these three levels plays a vital role in the success of the method. Miss out a level and the whole thing will come crashing down. Think of these three levels as the Holy Trinity of housework: each one is important in its own right, but put them all together and you have a pretty powerful combination. The levels are:

Level 1 Daily running tasks that you do throughout the day (totalling 15 minutes).

Level 2 This is the 30-minute routine that you adopt for Mondays to Thursdays.

Level 3 The Friday Focus, again of 30 minutes, where you concentrate on a different room each week for a deep tidy and clean.

Level 1

If you stop to think about the list of jobs that are included in level 1 (listed below), the chances are that you will doing a lot of them already in the day-to-day running of your home. These are the most basic of jobs that we should be doing anyway as we go along, so why have I included them here? Quite simply, because you might not be doing them efficiently, so I am going to help you to speed them up. These jobs exist *outside* your 30 minutes per day, but I have included them to give you a gentle nudge to do the basics that come with running a home. They will make sure that your whole home runs like a well-oiled machine and that the place stays looking lovely in between each room clean. Doing these will ensure that your 30 minutes' cleaning routine is much easier to tackle and you will achieve much more in the time. In our house, Mike tackles the level 1 jobs and I do the 30 minutes for that particular day. (Mike also does all of his own ironing – did I mention that I am very happily married!)

My suggestions for your level 1 jobs are below (but keep in mind that only you know your home and your family. You might need to adapt the list slightly to suit your lifestyle, and that is absolutely A-OK). As a guide, your level 1 jobs should be a super-quick top-level tidy, and you should aim to

LEVEL 1 JOBS

✓ Make the beds. If you have kids old enough to get involved, this can be delegated to them. I have a nifty little trick to help them do this more easily, but we'll cover that on page 102.

✓ Do one load of laundry. By this I mean wash, dry and put the clothes away. It is very important that you actually put clothes away when they are finished, or you'll end up with piles of washing.

✓ Very quickly clean the bathrooms.

✓ Vacuum or sweep the main traffic areas in your home. This should be a really quick task – there's no need to be getting under the furniture or into all the corners. The whole point of this is to keep on top of the dust and dirt. If you vacuum daily there will be less dirt on the floors being walked around the home.

✓ Keep on top of the kitchen as you go through your day.

spend no more than 15 minutes on them in total, spread over the day. The reason why these jobs are so fast when you are following TOMM is because you will be keeping on top of everything over the week in your daily 30 minutes, making them a breeze.

If you do these jobs every day, you will find yourself in a wonderful routine that just becomes second nature. Once you have this down pat, you can whizz through these without really having to think about them. It will be a case of maintenance, and they will soon become really light-touch jobs. Remember: the more you do it, the easier it will be to keep on top of everything.

A WORD ON BATHROOMS

Keeping on top of the bathrooms is a level 1 job, so you'll be in there each weekday; however, if your heart desires it, you can also clean them at the weekends. TOMM hinges on getting things done little and often, and the same applies to the bathroom. As part of your level 1 jobs I suggest doing something a little different in the bathrooms each day. One day I might mop the floors, the next I'll be cleaning the sink – little and often is my mantra. In the interests of full disclosure, I clean the loos daily.

Level 2: the 30 minutes golden rules

Before we get into the sheer genius that is the 30 minutes, I want you to read through the golden rules: these will ensure that you are as efficient as possible with your time.

1 **Use a timer** This is non-negotiable – it is not the time for a guesstimate. You might find that you severely underestimate, or heavily overestimate, the time that you have been polishing the banisters.

2 **Look at the list of jobs** detailed below as a pick-and-mix of suggested things that you can do. It is impossible for me to give you an exhaustive list of the jobs that you need to do in your living room or in your kitchen because I haven't seen your house, I don't know how your home functions and I don't know how many people live there. Have a look at the list and then add or take things away as necessary.

3 **Start with the most urgent jobs** Before you set the timer, have a look around the room that you are about to tackle. Make a mental note (or a written one, if you prefer) and have a plan of action.

4 **When you are in each room,** plan what you need to do for your Friday Focus. This way you will know what needs doing, and you can make use of your time as effectively as possible.

LEVEL 2:
MONDAY TO THURSDAY

Monday: living room

- ✓ Tidy away anything that doesn't belong
- ✓ Wash throws and pet bedding
- ✓ A quick window clean, get rid of finger marks
- ✓ Sofa dive (vacuum under cushions)
- ✓ Dust
- ✓ Vacuum
- ✓ Mop if you have hard floors

Tuesday: bedrooms (see note page 48)

- ✓ Strip beds
- ✓ Tidy away anything that doesn't belong
- ✓ Quick mine-sweep under beds
- ✓ Dust
- ✓ Vacuum
- ✓ Remake beds

Wednesday: entrance hall and stairs

- ✓ Tidy away anything that doesn't belong
- ✓ Dust
- ✓ Vacuum
- ✓ Mop if you have hard floors

Thursday: kitchen

✓ Empty the crumbs out of the toaster
✓ Clean the inside of the microwave
✓ Clean out the cutlery drawer(s)
✓ Quick fridge clean
✓ Dust the blinds
✓ Clean the windows
✓ Clean the splash-back behind the hob

✓ Clean the hob top
✓ Give the sink a really good scrub
✓ Wipe down all the working surfaces
✓ Wipe down the cupboard fronts
✓ Vacuum and mop

Friday: focus day

(See Friday Focus in detail on page 48)

My top tips to maximise your 30 minutes

Over the years I have been doing TOMM I have learnt some tricks that mean I can get as much done as possible in the time.

1 **Always set your timer** As explained earlier, this is the first rule and it's non-negotiable. If you have a competitive streak, you can always try to beat your previous time.

2 **Put a playlist on** Nothing puts fire into your duster like some good tunes. Clean to the beat and the 30 minutes will fly by.

3 **I always start in one corner** of the room and work my way round in a clockwise direction. This means that I am not flitting around all over the place wasting time. Moving around in an efficient way means that you will concentrate your efforts in a methodical fashion, you will get loads more done and you will feel much less flustered.

4 **When dusting start at the top** of the room and move your duster downwards. This way the dirt will fall down onto the next surface that you are about to tackle.

5 **Always dust before you vacuum** If you do it the other way round, you will be spreading dust all over the floor and you will have wasted your time vacuuming in the first place.

6 **If you can, try to invest in a good cordless vacuum cleaner** This will shave so much time off your cleaning, as you won't have to faff about unplugging and plugging it in again.

7 **Don't do the same jobs every week** Mix it up a bit – after all, variety is the spice of life. You know your own house, and if you know that something doesn't really need doing on a weekly basis, switch it out for another job next week. You are in control: your home, your rules.

8 **Don't get caught in the weeds** Don't spend your 30 minutes polishing all your photograph frames. You will get to the end of your time and not see a lot for your efforts.

9 **If you find that you get distracted easily** and have a tendency to aimlessly scroll through your phone, put on a pair of rubber gloves. They will help to focus your mind, because every time you look down you will see a huge pair of yellow hands that will scream *housework*! Wearing gloves also makes it a whole lot harder to use your phone.

10 **Prioritise** Make sure you know the jobs that need doing first so that you won't waste time procrastinating. Start with the urgent stuff and then work your way down the list. Always leave the mopping until last; mop yourself out of the room you are cleaning to avoid leaving messy footprints on the floor walking back and forth.

A NOTE ON BEDROOMS

Bedroom day is often the most challenging for TOMM newbies, but it gets easier – you just need to get into your grove. One tip is to have spare bedding ready so you can wash and dry those dirty sheets at your leisure.

Trust the process and TOMM. You will get faster and more efficient each week. I promise.

FRIDAYS – WHAT MAKES THEM SO SPECIAL?

We've got the 30 minutes Monday to Thursday licked. Now it is time to talk about Fridays and to ponder the way that Fridays are the cornerstone of TOMM. As explained earlier, on Fridays we go deeper and do a focus in one particular room. I call it the Friday Focus and it is the key to the whole shebang, because it guarantees that the main areas of your home get a deep clean on a regular basis. You will still only be doing it for 30 minutes, but because you will already have been in that room earlier on in the week, you will be able to get down to the nitty-gritty straight away without having to do a top-level tidy first.

Level 3: the Friday Focus

Once you have been following TOMM for a while you will see a very handy pattern emerging. When the time is drawing near for the Friday Focus in a certain room (let's use your kitchen as an example) you might start to notice areas that need a deeper clean, perhaps the oven is starting to look a bit uncared for or the underneath of your sink needs a good sort out. These jobs are tackled in the focus days and this means that you won't become overwhelmed with a huge list of jobs when you stare into the abyss of kitchen day. The harder jobs get their own day. By the way, don't get freaked out by the thought of cleaning your oven on kitchen Friday Focus. Later I will show you ways to keep your oven looking fab so that you don't have to spend hours up to your elbows in grease when it is time to clean it.

On week 3, when the kitchen is the focus area, this room will get double duty, one whole hour of cleaning: half an hour on Thursday and half an hour as the Friday Focus. And that is one of the reasons why TOMM works, your home will carry on getting cleaner and cleaner. You will be cleaning smarter, not harder and it will all seem so much easier to cope with.

The Friday Focus works on a rolling eight-week cycle, so if you are the kind of person who loves to join in with a community, or perhaps you work better in a team, all TeamTOMM members follow the same schedule. We are all on the same week together and that is where our amazing sense of community comes from. Of course, you don't have to wait until week 1 to start; you can jump in at any time. If you want to work along with TeamTOMM, head over to my social media pages and join in.

THE FRIDAY FOCUS CHECKLIST

Remember: 30 minutes only!

Week 1: the kids' rooms

- ✓ Toy cull
- ✓ Cull clothes that no longer fit
- ✓ Straighten shelves/ bookcases
- ✓ Clean windows and mirrors
- ✓ Dust skirting boards
- ✓ Vacuum under furniture

Week 2: living room

- ✓ Shampoo rugs
- ✓ Clean cushion covers
- ✓ Clean sofa covers if they are removable
- ✓ Dust skirting boards
- ✓ Vacuum under furniture

Week 3: kitchen

- ✓ Pick two or three cupboards to declutter
- ✓ Clean extractor fan filters
- ✓ Clean the oven
- ✓ Clean the kickboards

Week 4: bathrooms

- ✓ Tackle the limescale
- ✓ Clean out the bathroom cabinet
- ✓ Tackle the grout
- ✓ Clean the windows
- ✓ Deep-clean the floors

Week 5: master bedroom

✓ Quick clothes/make-up cull
✓ Clean windows and mirrors

✓ Dust the skirting boards
✓ Vacuum under furniture

Week 6: entrance hall and stairs

✓ Have a shoe/coat cull
✓ Go through lurking piles of paper
✓ Clean the banisters

✓ Clean the windows and mirrors
✓ Dust the skirting boards
✓ Vacuum under furniture
✓ Shampoo the rugs

Week 7: miscellaneous room

✓ Tidy away anything that does not belong/ declutter
✓ Clean the windows and mirrors

✓ Dust the skirting boards
✓ Vacuum under furniture

Week 8: garden/outside space

✓ Clean the front door/ doorstep
✓ Plant some seasonal flowers in pots

✓ Quick weed of flowerbed
✓ Sweep the patio
✓ Clean out the bin store

Remember: the Friday Focus is the key to TOMM.

CERYS'S STORY

I'm a shift worker and I am also studying at the same time. I don't have kids

My working situation is a funny one. I'm a mental health support worker, so I work about 25 hours a week on shifts, and I'm also studying social work full time at university. I live with my partner Tom and our two cats.

There's no such thing as a typical day in our household. Some days we are both out at work or uni, sometimes I'm in all day on my own or Tom is in on his own, and at other times we're both in all day together. It's never the same – that's the joy of shifts!

We fit TOMM in by sharing the responsibility. We have all our different levels of jobs printed out on a sheet and we get as much done as we can, ticking each one off as we go. Some get done in the morning and the rest will be finished in the evening.

TOMM helps me because I tend to over-obsess about cleaning. My very busy lifestyle means the cleaning can get overwhelming for me and, if I have no direction, I just over-clean (usually the wrong things!). Following TOMM ensures I only spend 30 minutes a day cleaning and it means my home always feel clean, which helps with my mental health. My partner also loves TOMM because he has a set list of things to do, so he knows exactly what needs doing each day. It has stopped any resentment from either of us if we feel we are doing more than the other – now we both just do as much as we can on the list every day.

My advice to newbies is to do the Boot Camp first. We had just moved into our first home when we came across TOMM and I didn't think we needed the Boot Camp, but the first couple of weeks took more than 30 minutes every day. Boot Camp will make your life easier. Secondly, it might take slightly longer when you first start out, but the longer you use the method the cleaner everything will become and the quicker you will get things done. And lastly, write up all the jobs you want to do and create a tick list. Being able to see what needs doing every day and ticking them off really helps. This also helps you think about bits of the house you might forget.

We also have an on-going list of things that we notice need to be added to the rota (for example, washing machine filters and vacuum filters). The Facebook group will be your bible – it's like a cleaning support group, where everyone is friendly and you can get any advice you need. Good luck!

3

How to be a Smooth Mover with Fast Cleaning

Are you a cleaning newbie? Are these your first tentative steps into the world of cleaning? Perhaps you have just moved out of home and you are not well versed in the world of dusters and vacuum cleaners. Do you feel overwhelmed when you look at the shelves in the cleaning aisle? Or would you just like to be more efficient with your cleaning?

I have got some really good news. Cleaning and keeping a home doesn't have to be complicated. You don't need to spend loads of money on products, nor do you have to have a chemistry degree in order to clean properly. Most of it is common sense and you can get away with cleaning most of your home with a basic kit that includes two or three cleaning products, hot soapy water, a vacuum cleaner, a mop, a few cloths and a long-handled duster. Everything else is just sprinkles on your cupcake. Start with the basics and you will learn the rest as you go along.

I will let you into a secret. The only person you are keeping your home clean for is you and the other people who live there. Don't do it for your health visitor, aunt, sister... Do it for you. The beauty of you being in control is that you can set your own standards. It is important to note here that everyone will have their own standards; this is totally OK and part of what makes us human.

Here are some basic room-by-room tips to help get you started. You will notice on the tick lists in the previous chapter that I have suggested jobs for you to do in each room, but these are not set in stone. I have also suggested an order for them to be done. I have done this to make sure that you are cleaning in the most efficient way possible. But remember that I have not been inside your house so I don't know the lie of the land.

Look at the list of jobs on the list as a pick-and-mix of things to do. Do what is applicable to your home. You can change what you do in each room each week and that is fine, too. All I would say is: always start with the most urgent jobs first and work your way through the list. And remember, always start in one corner and work your way around the room in a clockwise direction, it will keep you focused and on track.

THE LIVING ROOM

Here are some handy hints for that most important of rooms – the one we all want to keep looking (and smelling!) great.

HOW TO DUST

You might not think that there is an art to dusting, but if you do it the right way you will save yourself time and you will stop the dust from being spread all over the room.

I always try to damp-dust as much as I can around the home. Damp-dusting isn't as complicated as it sounds; it purely means that I use a damp cloth (usually a microfibre cloth) to wipe over surfaces. But, of course, you can make use of old tea towels or ripped-up old clothes. When you damp dust, you trap all the dust on the cloth, which stops it from being sent into the air in the room, and this makes it a great way to dust if you or anyone else in your house suffers from allergies.

When I dust, I start at the top of room and work my way down. Start with the cobwebs in the corners near the ceiling and then work your way towards the floor dusting anything that is in your path. This means that any dust that isn't trapped in your cloth will fall to the surface below, but that is OK because you are just about to dust there.

To get to the hard-to-reach areas or to dust tricky things, such as picture frames or ceiling lights, I prefer using the delicate touch of an ostrich feather duster. This might sound posh, but I like to think of it as my only cleaning indulgence.

Of course, another way to dust is to use the soft brush attachment on your vacuum cleaner (if you have one). This is particularly effective on skirting boards, air vents and around the back of electrical items such as computer towers.

It might seem obvious, but the less clutter you have in your room, the less you will need to dust, so keep that in mind when you acquire or shop for knick-knacks. My mum calls these 'dust collectors'. How right she is.

Sofas

Since sofas are not cheap, you need to make sure that you look after them. Keep your sofas and armchairs looking newer for longer by flipping and turning your sofa cushions on a regular basis (if the design of your sofa allows you to). This will mean that they will wear evenly, and you won't be left with that telltale groove where your bum fits nicely.

If you can, try to invest in washable sofa covers. We have had a white sofa for years, and the first thing that most people say when they come into our living room is that they can't believe how brave I am having for a white sofa, three kids and a dog. But while at first glance it might seem that I have slightly lost the plot, I can assure you that there is method in my madness. That is because I can take my sofa covers off and bung them in the washing machine at 60 degrees and this means that they are much easier to maintain than a fixed fabric sofa. Another great option is leather, as they can weather many a storm from kids and pets!

Windows

Many people battle with smeary windows, and sometimes, despite our best efforts to clean them, it only seems to make them worse. If you want windows that look like they are not actually there, the first thing you need to do is to tackle any product build-up that you might have. This is especially important if you have been trying out loads of lotions and potions to make your windows sparkle. One of the best ways of doing this I find is to use very hot soapy water. Use water as hot as you can stand, but always wear rubber gloves and be extra careful not to burn yourself. Any washing-up liquid will do; after all, if it is good enough for your crystalware then it will work just as well on your windows.

Once you have battled the build-up, head in there again with a fresh batch of hot soapy water and a clean cloth. Give the windows a really good clean, you will need a decent amount of elbow grease for this, but make sure that you don't over-wet the windows, or it will make drying them harder. When you dry them, you can either use a microfibre cloth especially for windows or you can use newspaper (this is a trick that I learnt in the chip shops). Buff them up really well with a downwards, zigzag motion until they are dry and sparkly. You will know you are doing it properly because it will become an arm workout.

A great way to maintain your windows is with a 50/50 vinegar-and-water solution and a really good buff (as above).

THE BEDROOMS

'Bedroom day', or 'clean-sheet Tuesday' as it has become affectionately known by TeamTOMM, can be a bit like Marmite: you either love it or hate it. One thing is for sure, though, you will love the feeling of getting into clean sheets at the end of the day and that, for most people, is enough motivation to push them towards the finish line.

The beds

I nearly always split up my 30 minutes on Tuesdays. First thing in the morning we strip all the beds (the older two boys are in charge of stripping theirs) and we get the sheets in the washing machine early. I usually do two loads of washing on bedroom day (one load with the kids' sheets and another load with the sheets from the master bedroom). Once they are washed and I have put them on an extra spin (this is a top tip for reducing drying times, but more on this on page 144), I can either hang them on the washing line, if the weather is playing ball, or start drying them in the tumble dryer. I will then start on the rest of my bedroom jobs and do my 30 minutes, but I will always leave a few minutes spare, so that I can remake the beds when the sheets are dry later in the day.

A little heads up: there is nothing worse than climbing up the stairs to bed at the end of a long day to find that there are no sheets on the bed because you've forgotten to make it. Be your future friend and get them onto the bed before you get too tired. (You will find more about being your future friend on page 106.) Of course, if you have more than one set of bedding for each bed, there is no need for you to wait for your bedding to dry before you complete your 30 minutes. Just pop the new set on straight away and then all you have to do is fold and store the rest when it is dry.

GEM'S TOP TIP

 Store bedding sets in a pillowcase from its matching set. It will keep everything together in a nice easy-to-grab bundle, and it will look super-organised in your cupboard.

One of the best ways to keep your bedroom smelling fresh is to air it every single day. I do this by pulling the duvet back and opening the windows wide while we are milling around the house in the morning (just make sure you're dressed or you'll scare the neighbours!). I even do this in the winter, and it can be argued that doing this is in the winter is even more important than in the summer because your home is sealed tight during the day to keep the heat in. In the summer, windows are opened frequently to keep the house cool. Every morning we air the bedrooms while we are getting ready to leave the house and this helps to banish that musty 'people have slept in here' smell. Letting your home breathe is a vital step to help it keep smelling fresh as a daisy.

Remember to wash your pillows and duvets regularly (see overleaf for tips on washing pillows). If your washing machine has a large enough drum, then you might be able to do this at home, but if you have a launderette near you they may be able to do it for you.

Obviously, pillows don't live forever, so a top tip is to fold them in half, and if they spring back into shape they still have some life left in them. If they stay folded or just generally look like they have seen better days, now is the time for them to be replaced.

HOW TO WASH PILLOWS

- Pillows need washing at least every six months (more regularly if you live in a hot climate), and the good news is that they are a lot easier to wash than most people think.

- Most pillows can be washed in the washing machine, but always err on the side of caution and check the washing instructions before you blunder ahead.

- If you have very delicate pillows, it might be wise to wash them on the hand-wash cycle on your machine (as this will keep the spin cycle low and prevent them from becoming damaged).

- I usually wash two pillows at a time and dry two at a time, this helps to keep the washing machine and the tumble dryer balanced.

- When the pillows are clean, give them a really good thumping. This will help them get back into their pillow-like shape. There is nothing worse than ending up with a knobbly pillow.

- Now place them in the tumble dryer on a low setting. (I throw in a couple of clean tennis balls to help to reshape them).

Mattresses need turning approximately twice a year, and a nice way to remember this is to do it at the turning of the seasons in summer and winter. In order to keep your mattress as fresh as possible (and to combat things like dust mites), you need to vacuum it regularly, and, if you have one, you can use a steam cleaner on the upholstery setting to keep it fresh.

We know that you can't clean clutter so for this reason it is important to keep bedrooms as clutter free as possible. The Friday focus in the kids' rooms and the master bedroom will help you keep on top of this.

THE HALLWAY AND STAIRS

I know that the TOMMers who live in three-storey houses are not big fans of Wednesdays, but on the flip side, the bungalow dwellers are in their element when Wednesday rolls around. If hallway day is an easy day for you, you might like to incorporate some catch-up time. Wednesday can be your safety net for any other jobs that you might have missed over the week.

Invest in a good doormat, as this will trap most of the dirt before it can be trodden into the house. Of course, it is totally up to you whether or not you are a shoes-off or shoes-on household (we are shoes-off), but I find that it is much more practical to have hard floors downstairs, as they are much easier to clean and, if you have guests, they can keep their shoes on if they want to. There's nothing worse than insisting someone takes their shoes off. It makes people feel uncomfortable. I only enforce the shoes-off rules for family members. I'm nice like that.

THE KITCHEN

One of the best ways that I like to tackle grease in the kitchen is by using old-school hot soapy water. It is a miracle worker. If you think about, it washing-up liquid is made to tackle greasy, dirty dishes, so it stands to reason that it will do a fab job cleaning all the greasy surfaces in your kitchen. I like to use it on the splashback behind the hob, on the worktops and on my stainless steel cooker top. As always, remember to check manufacturer's instructions to ensure you do not damage any surfaces.

Take on your oven (and win)

Oven cleaning: hands up who loves this job? Anyone? No, didn't think so. But oven cleaning is something that will crop up from time to time, and most TOMMers tackle this on their Friday Focus. But before you say, 'There is no way I can clean my oven in 30 minutes' let me tell you how you can keep on top of it so that you are never faced with a mammoth oven clean ever again.

If you haven't got them in the base of your oven, then I urge you to get yourself some oven liners. Not only are they as cheap as chips, but they will also become invaluable to you when you see just how easy they make keeping the base of your oven clean. Oven liners will sit at the bottom of your oven and catch any spills that occur; think about that bubbling-over lasagne that has usually become encrusted onto

the bottom of your oven by the time you get around to cleaning it. Because oven liners are non-stick, all you need to do is
wash them under the tap, dry them off and pop them back in
your oven (it takes seconds). They are seriously life changing.
No more chipping away at burnt on food for hours on end.
Do check it is safe to use oven liners in your oven.

For the rest of your oven – the glass and the racks – you
can save yourself having to scrub them by wiping them down
while they are still warm. Make sure that the oven isn't hot,
or you will burn yourself. Once it has cooled down enough
for you to get in there, use some hot soapy water and wipe
down all the splashes before they have a chance to solidify.

If you have a stainless steel oven and you want to keep it
shiny for as long as possible in between cleans, all you need
is a tiny bit of baby oil and a cloth. Use it to buff up clean
stainless steel and it will bring it up to a marvellous shine and
keep it looking that way for longer. But remember to use only
a tiny drop of oil, as a little goes a long way.

Washing machine and dishwasher

Thank God for these two. I often think back to my nana's
house where she still had her old-fashioned mangle and I
ponder how hard washing must have been back in the day
before domestic duties were made so much easier by tech-
nology. But, as with all things, in order for the washing
machine and the dishwasher to perform at their best, they
need a bit of TLC.

I like to run both my dishwasher and my washing machines on their highest cycles every couple of weeks, and I do this with a cupful of white vinegar. I live in a hard water area, so their pipes deserve a bit of a spa day every now and again. Doing this will help to get rid of any limescale and keep your machines sparkling and running efficiently.

Leave the door of your washing machine slightly open when it is not in use. This will make sure that air can circulate, stopping mildew build-up, which can cause a stinky machine and a mouldy seal (something which none of us want).

Also, remember to pay attention to the filters, and make sure they are not getting clogged up, with regular filter cleaning sessions. Thinking of prevention rather than cure, always be your future friend and check pockets before you put clothing into the washing machine.

Tumble dryer

If you are lucky enough to have a tumble dryer, you also need to maintain it. It is absolutely vital that you remove the lint and fluff from the filter after each use, as when this builds up it becomes a fire hazard.

THINGS THAT YOU MIGHT BE FORGETTING TO CLEAN IN THE KITCHEN

- The crumb catcher in the toaster. This is where the raisins from your fruit loaf go to die.

- The seal around your fridge and freezer. This can often go neglected, but it is so satisfying to clean.

- The cutlery drawer tray. I like to do this every couple of weeks. I don't know how it gets so dusty in there.

- The extractor fan filters. Mine can go in the dishwasher; check to see if yours can too.

- The kitchen cupboard kickboards. Ask yourself when was the last time you got on your hands and knees and gave them a good scrub? Clean kickboards are a great way to bring a dull kitchen back to life again.

THE BATHROOMS

Bathroom cleaning is a hot topic in TeamTOMM. I promise that they aren't as scary to clean properly as people think, and if you make sure that you approach bathroom cleaning with a little-and-often mindset, you will always be on top of them. I change what I do in there on a daily basis and, if you do the same, you will be always be one step ahead. Remember: because they are part of your level 1 tasks, this is your friendly reminder to give them some TLC daily.

Bathroom cleaning is a bit more than the loo and the sink, however, so I thought I would write a handy little list just as a reminder of the most forgotten areas of the bathroom when it comes to getting them looking all sparkly and keeping the bathroom a room that you can be proud of.

1   **Don't forget to clean the light switches**/light pulls. In fact, these are often forgotten about all over the house, so be sure to have them on your radar.

2   **The toilet flush handle** needs to be cleaned too. This is really important. Just take a moment to think of the order that people do things in the loo. They use the loo, flush the loo then wash their hands. Enough said (sorry if you are eating).

3   **Don't neglect the toilet pedestal** and the pipe at the back of the loo. In order for the toilet to be properly clean, you need to get behind the toilet. And the same applies to the sink pedestal – these can get really grubby.

4   **A word about toothbrush holders** We got rid of ours years ago. Quite simply, they can collect water from your toothbrushes and this all collects at the bottom of the holder; if left unchecked, it can start to go very manky and become a breeding ground for germs and general gunk. We have electric toothbrushes that are able to stand up unaided, so there is no need for a toothbrush holder.

5   **I have similar feelings towards toilet brush holders** – we don't have toilet brushes. They make me feel even worse than toothbrush holders. But if you don't feel the same way, then you must clean them and the holder regularly, we all know why this is. People often ask me how I clean my toilet if I don't have a toilet brush, and the truth is that if you clean it daily you will reduce the risk of having to give it a really good scrub. I find rubber gloves, toilet cleaner and a cloth is all you need.

6   **Extractor vents** – they are absolute dust traps. Pay attention to them every now and again. A good way to clean them is to get your cordless vacuum out and use the duster attachment.

7   **If you are battling with limescale**, a solution of half white vinegar and half water is a great way to get rid of it. You can also soak your showerhead in it to unclog it and make it work like new again.

8   **If you are using vinegar for cleaning**, be sure not to use it on surfaces such as granite, marble or natural stone, as it can damage them. Always check your surfaces are suitable for a certain product before you steam in – you don't want to damage them. (See also page 73 for safety when using vinegar and bleach.)

9   **Mould and mildew** One of the most effective ways to stop them building up is to allow fresh air into your bathroom, so open up the windows and let the steam out.

10 **Tiles and shower screen** To keep these looking sparkly for longer, give them a quick wipe down after use.

4

Cleaning in Natural Ways

Unless you have been living under a rock lately you will have noticed the rise in the popularity of eco-friendly cleaning products. TeamTOMM are all over it on the Facebook group and I have been fascinated to watch the topic open up on social media. It seems that in the past few months the subject has been blown right open, and more people are trying to cut down on single-use plastic and unnecessary cleaning chemicals in their homes.

Wherever you are on your eco journey, be it right at the start or a few steps down the line, I have some hints and tips that will help you be more environmentally conscious in your home. Last year I spent a whole week using purely environmentally friendly cleaning products. I called it my eco week. I had never ventured into the eco-friendly cleaning section of the supermarket before and these were unchartered waters. But I put on my big girl pants and in the interests of a good old-fashioned experiment I blogged about my findings.

One of the most startling things I found was that when I ditched the artificially enhanced fragrances, my home actually smelt cleaner and the air felt fresher. So much so that when I returned to some of my tried-and-trusted old faithfuls, I found their smell overpowering, and that was only after one week. Lots of members of TeamTOMM who have fully made the shift to environmentally friendly cleaning products tell me that your nose soon gets used to the subtler smell of natural cleaners and they now find commercially produced cleaners too strong.

Since then I have been learning about and researching greener cleaning solutions. I have tried some things that didn't work and others that have knocked my socks off when it comes to their cleaning power. And you might be surprised to know that most of the things that work the best are the old-school methods. It seems that we might have been overdoing it again. The great thing about many eco-cleaning tips is that not only will they help you save the planet one loo clean at a time, but they will also help you to save some cash too. Many of them cost pennies. The Internet is full to bursting with eco-friendly cleaning tips and it is fun trying them all out, but here are my favourites to save you a bit of legwork.

GEM'S TOP ECO-HOUSEKEEPING TIPS

1 **Number one has to be white vinegar**, white vinegar, white vinegar! This is one of the most powerful and versatile cleaning products that I have in my eco-cleaning caddy, and the best thing is that it costs next to nothing. Vinegar can be used to help with all sorts of things, including limescale. A quick google will open up a whole world of possibilities. I use it regularly on a hot wash through my dishwasher and washing machine to keep them running smoother for longer (a bit like a vinegar spa).

2 **Ditch the wipes** One of the best ways that you can cut down on waste is to stop using disposable antibacterial wipes in the home – and also ditch the disposable dishcloths. I made the transition a while ago to old-fashioned dishcloths and I haven't looked back. If you are worried about getting them clean, this is nothing that a boil wash can't fix.

3 **A great way to clean and refresh your wooden chopping board** is to cut a lemon in half, sprinkle some coarse salt on it and then rub it over the board to deodorise it.

4 **If you are looking for a way to deodorise your carpets and rugs**, then bicarbonate of soda is your friend. You can either use it to sprinkle straight onto your carpet or you can mix it with your favourite essential oil. Leave it for about 30 minutes and vacuum it up. If you are using essential oils, please make sure that you are using ones that are safe around children and pets.

▶

5 **Ditch the artificial air fresheners** and open your windows. This is hands down one of the best ways to keep your home smelling as fresh as a daisy, and it is even more important to do it in the winter.

6 **One of the best ways to reduce the number of products** that you use is to increase the amount of elbow grease you put into your cleaning. Cleaning products don't get rid of dirt alone, the scrubbing action also helps. If you ramp this up, you can dial down on your use of the product.

7 **Take it one step at a time**: making the switch is much less overwhelming if you make one small change at a time.

8 **If making your own cleaning products is a step too far** for you right now, consider to switching to eco-friendlier shop-bought cleaning products. Most supermarkets are catching on to the new wave and are producing their own versions. (The Waitrose ECOlogical range is a must try.) Other companies, such as Splosh, are producing refillable bottles so that you can drastically reduce your plastic waste.

CLEANING AND HEALTH

You might be switching to more eco-friendly products not just to help the planet but for health benefits too. Homemade cleaning products are much kinder, not only to the environment, but also to our bodies. It is obvious that the more cleaning products we use in our homes, the more chemicals we are releasing into the air we breathe, and that is not good. It can be very tempting when you start your cleaning journey to become carried away and use too many products. Although you might have a gleaming kitchen, the air in your home is now full of chemicals that you are breathing in – the difference is you just can't see it.

As with most things in life, a common-sense, balanced approach has to be applied. You can have too much of a good thing. Just as I was cleaning too much in the past, it is totally possible to use too many cleaning products. At best it can be a complete waste of time and money, and at worst it can be damaging to your health. It is vital that you always read the instructions to make sure that you are using them in the correct and safe way. You need to do this to stop yourself (and the people you live with) from coming to any harm.

As well as always following the instructions on the products, you need to make sure you practise safe cleaning and never mix cleaning products. This is because some cleaning chemicals can produce harmful effects when they are mixed together. Did you know that mixing vinegar and bleach can produce chlorine gas? Something I am guessing you don't want floating around your home.

But it is very easily done. It is easy to fall into the trap of thinking that doubling up on cleaning products will get the job done better and faster. Let's say, for example, that you are cleaning the bathroom and you have cleaned your shower screen with a water-and-vinegar mix. It has been dripping down onto your shower-screen seal, which is also dirty, so you decide to clean that too. You put some bleach on the seal, but ... remember: bleach + vinegar = chlorine gas

Always practise safe cleaning; read the instructions, use products only as they are intended and protect yourself and your family.

PART 2

Make TOMM Work For You

5

Fit TOMM Around Your Working Week

The beauty of TOMM is that it is flexible and this means that you can bend it and shape it to fit in with your life. TOMM is not a rigid routine that forces you to try to shove a square peg into a round hole. It is fully adaptable to suit your lifestyle. And as your life changes, or you have kids, change jobs or move house, you can take it with you, safe in the knowledge that it can handle pretty much anything you throw at it.

The way TOMM is structured also means that you will never again be faced with a full day of cleaning to catch up with the stuff you have missed over the week. No more wasted weekends. You will no longer be getting up close and personal with your duster on a Sunday; you will have more time to get the chance of a lie-in or have a relaxing bath – or just treat yourself to a chill-out day without any of the guilt.

I totally understand that when you are working and

looking after kids, *and* managing a home, you can feel really overwhelmed. It feels as though there is always something else to do, like a never-ending to-do list. When I was working in the fish and chip shops, I would get up with the kids in the morning and get them ready for the day (take them to pre-school, and so on) and then carry on my merry way to start prepping for the lunchtime service at the chip shop. I would get to work about 10am and, on my long shifts, I would not get home until 10pm. Working in catering is fun, and every single day is different, but the days are long, and the hours are not at all social.

My days were tiring, and I would be on my feet for most of them, but I still did TOMM. Otherwise, it would mean that my only full day off (which was Sunday) would have been spent cleaning. It was a challenging time, but for the most part I managed to be my future friend. This is how I did it.

MY EARLY ROUTINE

Because I didn't need to be at work until 10am, I would fit in 15 minutes of housework when I first got up (which was early because at the time I had two children under three years) and then the last 15 minutes later on in the morning. This meant that I wasn't overwhelmed with a 30-minute chunk of house-work before a 12-hour shift. Psychologically somehow, when you split the time up, it doesn't seem as daunting.

I haven't only worked in fish and chip shops, however. I have also worked nine to five in an office, spent some very fun years as an antenatal teacher (which meant lots of evening and weekend work) and I have worked as a doula, which meant that when I had a client I would be on 24-hour call for a four-week period. Throughout all this I found a way to make TOMM work. In fact, it has been one of the only things in my life that has remained constant. TOMM always had my back.

YOU CAN SWAP THE DAYS AROUND

If you work shifts, full-time or even part-time, you might need to sit down and give TOMM a bit of a tweak. If Tuesdays are your busiest day of the week, and you know that you will not be able to give clean-sheet Tuesday the attention it deserves, feel free to swap it over for an easier day. Wednesday (or hallway day, as I now call it) is traditionally the easiest day for me, so if this works better for you, swap the two around.

TOMM is not prescriptive; you won't get a rap on the knuckles from me if you do clean-sheet Monday. It is honestly much more important to me that it works for as many people as possible. You have to make it work for you, and while (on the whole) most people stick to the days that I have suggested, there are also loads of TOMMers who have modified the method to make it rock for them.

You have to remember that when I sat down at my kitchen table 12 years ago and I came up with TOMM, I was never expecting that one day so many of you would be following along too. When I devised it, I devised it to suit myself and my lifestyle. It was my little private coping mechanism.

THE REASONING BEHIND TOMM'S STRUCTURE

Quite a bit of thought went into why I chose the specific days for each room. Here is why I chose the routine as it is today:

Monday The first day back from the weekend and the living room will have probably got a bit of a bashing over Saturday and Sunday (especially if you have kids), so the primary focus at the start of the week is to get this room looking at its best again.

Tuesday Because bedroom day can be a bit more of a difficult day, that is why it isn't on a Monday (because Mondays are bad enough as it is), and also if it is later in the week, energy levels might be starting to flag.

Wednesday – for me, and many others, it's the worst and most boring day of the week, so I made it hallway day because the hall never seems to take that long and it therefore seems like a bit of a day off. Wednesdays no longer seem that bad any more.

Thursday This was designated as kitchen day because who doesn't want a decent-looking kitchen when they down tools on Friday ready for the weekend? Plus, Friday is no-cook Friday in our house, meaning that the kitchen will stay looking fab for longer.

Friday The focus day was given to Friday because, as well as the obvious alliteration that was just too good an opportunity to pass up, the thought of a housework-free weekend gives just the right amount of impetus to get it done.

That is the madness behind the method. As long as you stick to the basic principles of 30 minutes a day you'll still be rocking the housework.

VICTORIA'S STORY

I have three children and run my own business

I was a young mum; a teenage mum from a difficult home life. I had been caring for my own mum since I was a child, as well as my two younger brothers, and getting pregnant at 16 seemed just another part of my life. After my son was born we moved a lot, sometimes to a flat or bed and breakfast and at other times to someone's spare room. Fast-forward two years and I was married and settled, living in my first real home with baby number two on the way.

Did I have a clue how to manage my home? No. Did I have realistic goals? Nope! The flat would either be pristine after hours and hours of cleaning or be the other extreme, with the sink overflowing and no one able to find clean clothes.

Ten years on I'm still happily married, but now have three wonderful children and my own business. I also home educate my children. Over the last few years the pressure I put on myself to keep the house tidy grew and grew. I would spend days cleaning, making myself ill only for it to all fall apart. And not once did I ever feel in control of the laundry.

Three months ago, a friend mentioned The Organised Mum Method. At first, I got defensive, saying, 'I'm fine!' and 'I can't commit to a schedule, I'm far too busy.' I don't really know what happened to make me try – it might have been the tick-list idea. The Week 1 Boot Camp was tough and, if I'm honest, I had no idea how I would ever get it down to 30 minutes a day. But I kept going and asked my husband to hold me accountable if I missed a day.

Three months on, my house is tidy, we are always on top of the laundry and everyone looks forward to Clean Sheet Tuesday! The house isn't perfect but it's clean, and I know that by Friday everything will have had a good going-over again, so I can have the weekend just for me.

The biggest bonus was last week. I hurt my back pretty badly and was virtually immobile for a few days. With some help from the family we actually stayed on top of TOMM, without it feeling like a chore. In times gone by when my back was bad it would have resulted in chaos in the house.

6

Using TOMM When Pregnant

If you have found TOMM for the first time and you are pregnant or finding that pregnancy isn't the romantic bubble that you had hoped for, or if you're still trying to function while having to run to the loo to be sick every ten minutes, fear not. I have trodden this path before, and I have found some tips to help you on your way. I have three kids, and each time I was pregnant I never bloomed. What I did do was throw up – a lot – so I do understand the problems that you might face.

It can be especially tricky when you have older kids and you are trying to spoon-feed mashed banana and sing 'The Wheels on the Bus' to a toddler when all you want to do is go to bed and sleep for one thousand years. Add housework to this and you are going to be one tired human. That is why it is totally OK to go into survival mode during pregnancy when it comes to housework. Just do what you need to do on a daily basis to keep everything ticking over. Accept as many offers of help as you can, and don't ever feel guilty about taking time out to rest. Now is not the time to start ramping up the cleaning, unless of course you are in the later stages of pregnancy and are starting to nest. In which case you might actually enjoy making your home ready for your impending new arrival. Gotta love those hormones!

If you are not feeling your best, this is not the time to have a massive declutter. Keep the cogs turning, but don't put pressure on yourself to have a Pinterest-worthy home. We know by now that going after a show home is a fool's errand – settle with good enough.

You might find yourself having aversions to strong smells, so now might be the perfect time to look into less toxic cleaning products. You might want to do this when the baby arrives too. Experiment with old-fashioned methods that will be kinder on the nose. Hot soapy water works wonders, for example. (See also my suggestions in Chapter 4.)

Always work to your ability Never overdo it or push yourself beyond what feels comfortable. If you are in the first stages of pregnancy and feel as though you need to go to bed every day at four o'clock, there really is no point in fighting it. Your body needs rest, so stick to the most urgent jobs and stop as soon as you need to.

Split your 30 minutes into smaller, more manageable portions. Either two 15-minute chunks or three 10-minute chunks. This way you will conserve your energy and the cleaning won't seem as overwhelming.

Break up the bigger jobs into smaller tasks. A massive mountain of laundry can be really daunting. Tackle it one stage at a time: fold it, then stop; a little while later, put it away. It makes it seem much less of an ordeal.

Always accept help when offered. This rule also applies to when you have had your baby. There are no medals in any part of parenthood for running yourself into the ground and getting ill.

Be your future friend Take advantage of the days when you have more energy and use this time to catch up or get ahead on tasks.

Don't feel pressured to get absolutely everything ready for the baby before he or she makes their appearance. The shops will still be open after you have had your baby. Don't bust your buttons to be 100 per cent ready – take your time and relax. Having a baby isn't like Christmas: the shops don't close.

As an extension to the last point, newborns sleep *a lot* Perhaps not at night when you want them to, but during the day they will feed/sleep/poo/feed/poo/sleep, so you will find yourself with time to do stuff (if you feel up to it), so bear this in mind, and perhaps save some easy projects for after the baby is born. Unless, of course, they have colic, in which case you probably won't have time to even go to the toilet in peace.

In the later stages of pregnancy getting on your hands and knees and dusting the skirting boards is a good thing as it can help your baby to get into a really good position for the birth. Keep this piece of info to yourself, though, just in case you can't be bothered.

Remember the golden rule: don't stand when you can sit, and don't sit when you can lie down. The message behind this is: grab any chance to rest while you still can.

Invest in a slow cooker Keeping yourself nourished when you feel queasy or too exhausted to cook can be challenging. Take a look at the slow cooker recipe section of this book starting on page 182, and find some go-to recipes. Some of them take seconds to prep, and this means that at the end of the day when the energy levels are flagging you will have something to eat.

Don't panic if the nesting instinct never happens – the pregnancy stereotypes are just that – stereotypes. Always work to your ability, and never do anything that doesn't feel right.

And finally, always remember the most important thing of all: if anything feels uncomfortable, then stop.

7

TOMM When You Have a Baby

I know what it's like when you suddenly have a new little person to look after. Your whole perspective shifts and your primary focus moves away from making sure everything is just right for their arrival, to caring for and nurturing the little human that you have created. It is just human nature. In the first few weeks, you will, no doubt, be operating in survival mode, and you will be very reactive to your new baby's needs. I remember it feeling very much as if I were living in a bubble – like I was walking around with my fingers in my ears and the rest of the world was slightly muffled as I, and my hormones, concentrated on being a mum. Nothing throws life into disarray quite like a newborn: they might be tiny, but they are powerful.

The most important thing to remember at this stage is that you need to prioritise the health of yourself and your newborn baby. This means that you need to ask for as much help as possible from family and friends while you are settling down to life with your new addition. This might mean, for example, that your partner takes on additional housework or other tasks or that you accept the help of a neighbour or friend to take your older child to school. Accept help when it is offered.

JUGGLING, AS A NEW MUM

After the initial few weeks of motherhood the bubble will naturally pop, and you will feel ready to join the hustle and bustle of the real world again. You might be at this stage right now, and this might be why you have reached for this book. This was the whole reason why I started TOMM in the first place. A brand-new baby threw my world into chaos and meant that I no longer had the luxury of time to get the housework done. In the months prior to the birth, even though I was working, I was able to take my time to do the housework as and when I needed to. I didn't have to think about fitting it around a baby or having to deal with the extra work involved. How is it possible for one tiny human to need so much stuff?

They say, 'Sleep when the baby sleeps', but when does the dusting get done? Not only was I finding it more challenging to fit everything in, but I was also very aware that my actions in the home would have a direct impact on the health and well-being of my new baby. I felt under a lot of pressure to get it all done, but I had so little time, what with the feeding, the changing, the feeding, the changing and the rocking to sleep. It left very little time for eating and looking after myself, let alone looking after my home to the standard I thought I needed to now I was a mum. Please do not fall into the same trap and think you have to be super-efficient at all times.

I wanted the dream. I had been sold such a perfect image of motherhood: pristine white linen sheets in a Moses basket, a contented rosy-cheeked baby sleeping while I did some postnatal yoga, and so on. Gah! This wasn't my reality, but I fought hard to make it so, and I drove myself into the ground trying to. It wasn't possible and something had to break, but I recognised (luckily) that I had to stop putting myself under so much pressure or that something would have been me.

I completely understand that you will be pulled in all directions. You won't have enough hours in the day, and when your baby is asleep she will most probably be sleeping on you, so you won't be able to jump up and do a load of washing. And, let's face it, you probably won't have the energy to do this either.

DON'T BE OVER-AMBITIOUS

The best plan of action when you have a new baby is to do things gradually. This phase won't last forever, even though it seems like it, and right now you need to concentrate on keeping the wheels turning and not turning your house into a palace of gleaming glory.

Also, remember: the newborn phase is not the time to jump head first into the Boot Camp. If having a baby has been the catalyst to making you want to take charge of the housework once and for all, I recommend that you take it very slowly. The last thing you want to do is pull out the entire contents of a wardrobe while your little darling is napping only to have to abandon it 5 minutes afterwards because the next feed is calling. Because who knows when you'll get the chance to finish it?

When new parents come to me and ask for advice I always give them these little golden rules to live by.

- Start one job at a time.
- Complete as much as you can of this job in 5 to 10-minute chunks (set the timer if you need to). You will be surprised at how much you can get done.
- Once you have completed your task, you can then decide if you want to move on to the next one.
- This applies to your 30 minutes. Split the 30 minutes into manageable chunks of time. If it freaks you out to stare down the barrel of half an hour of housework, break it up. Jobs never really take as long as we think, and you will feel a much greater sense of achievement ticking things off slowly throughout the day.

HOW WOULD THIS WORK IN A REAL-LIFE SITUATION?

It is 7am and your baby has been up feeding since 4am due to a growth spurt. You have a toddler who needs to be at preschool for 9am and you are not dressed yet – what do you do?

The first thing to do is to make sure that the two young ones are fed and settled. Then you have your shower. *Always* prioritise yourself over your home. One of the surest ways to lose yourself in parenthood is to put yourself last.

Once you are washed and dressed (and you have eaten – vital) you can now start to think about whether or not you have the energy and the time to tackle your level 1 jobs. As we know, level 1 jobs will take you approximately 15 minutes. The beauty of these jobs is that they amount to a top-level tidy only. When you are doing these jobs, the idea is that you don't allow yourself to get bogged down by detail. If you can't spare a full 15 minutes, perhaps just pick the most urgent job, which is usually either the bathrooms or the vacuuming. Anything that you can tick off the list this early in the morning is a major win. Plus, by choosing a small job, it is not the end of the world if one of your kids needs you. If your name is called, merely down tools and pick up where you left off when you can.

THE 30 MINUTES IN REALITY

The 30 minutes can seem really daunting, especially if you are lacking in energy and motivation after doing a mammoth session of night feeds. Hello cluster feeds.

New parents need to look at the suggested list of jobs and begin with the most urgent ones. Start with the most necessary jobs; after all, you don't know how much time you are going to have, so you don't want to be faffing around dusting your blinds when the hob needs a blooming good scrub.

If your baby needs you 10 minutes into your 30 minutes and you have started with the most urgent jobs then at least you will have got the basics done. And if your day unravels completely and you can't face any more cleaning then don't worry, you have done your best and kept the cogs turning.

ROUTINES AND BABIES

I know this won't come as a surprise to you, but when I had my first baby I was desperate to get into some sort of routine – and fast! Believe it or not, I recorded my baby's day on a spreadsheet; it was colour coded and everything. I tracked his feeding, sleeping and playing for a whole week in the desperate hope that I could look at the spreadsheet in my sleep-deprived slightly frazzled state and see a pattern in the colours. Needless to say it didn't happen.

What I actually discovered (and this was also what I found three children later and after years working as an antenatal teacher and doula) was that babies find their own routines. And at first you have to let go of the control and let the routine form naturally around you. It will happen; it might take a few weeks or so, but soon you will notice that things are happening at similar times of the day. This is when you can sit back and take stock of how you want your days to work. If you work better in the morning and you know that you will feel better mentally if you have ticked off your to-do list before lunch, see if there is a way that you can make this happen. If you prefer to wait until the evenings (perhaps when your partner is home to help or when the kids are asleep) and you can get a whole uninterrupted 30 minutes, this will work as well. Everybody is different, every family and every baby. You need to work out what fits best with your family.

What's more, putting on a pair of headphones and listening to music, an audio book or a podcast is a great way to zone out and practise some mindfulness and self-care. Typically, though, as soon as you are coasting away in a nice routine, your baby will move on to another developmental milestone and it will all shift again. The joy of kids – they certainly keep us on our toes.

To recap, and because I know you will be tired and some of the above will not have gone in:

- Don't bite off more than you can chew. Do one job at a time.
- Pick the most urgent jobs first.
- Always set the timer.
- Look after yourself.

8

How to Get Everyone Pitching In

One of the most common questions I get asked about keeping it all together is, 'How do I do this when the other people I live with make it all a mess again?' As mentioned earlier, the truth is that sometimes you can clean your home and then five minutes later the kids run rampage through the house and it looks as if you haven't bothered, so you stop bothering altogether. I totally get this, and I see cries for help daily from new members of TeamTOMM who are tearing their hair out at how fast all their good work can be undone.

First, though, I need you to look at things from a slightly different perspective. Trust me, I know how frustrating it can be when you feel as though you are carrying out most of the domestic delegation.

LEARNING NEW HABITS AND BREAKING OLD ONES

If you are just starting your TOMM journey, it might be the case that your family has never seen you act this way before. They might have seen you do a mammoth clean at the weekend and then see no cleaning for the rest of the week. Or perhaps they might need a bit of time to get used to the new way of doing things. You will need to set people's expectations that you are now planning on doing a little bit each day and, what's more, you are expecting everyone to pull their weight. This is only fair. It would be unrealistic for you to turn up to breakfast one morning and announce over the cereal that you were implementing a new housekeeping method and that everyone had to join in – and no excuses.

Start by sitting everyone down and explaining in a positive way why you want to do TOMM.

- Instead of saying, 'You need to help me, or I won't take you to the park/cinema/bowling', try 'If you help me do these jobs, I will have more time to take you to do fun stuff.'

- And instead of, 'I always do all the housework *and* I work full-time!', try 'I really need your help because I am finding everything a bit much.'

Sometimes a slight shift in the tone of a sentence can make all the difference. If you approach the running of your home like a team (after all, you all live in and enjoy the home), it will make a massive difference. Make it a team effort and it can achieve two things:

1 It will stop one person from shouldering the full responsibility of the housework.

2 If you get the kids involved it will teach them vital life skills for the future. Leading by example is a great way to teach children, so be the change that you want to see and make sure that all the other adults in the household are on board.

When you free yourself from the burden of being the domestic delegator, a huge weight of responsibility will be lifted from your shoulders. And this is where the beauty of the tick lists in Chapter 2 and the printable charts come in (these are free to download on my blog). Once printed out and proudly displayed on the fridge, everyone will know where they stand and will be able to see at a glance what jobs need to be done on what day, what has already been ticked off and how they can pull their weight. This means no gentle nudges, no asking and, best of all, *no arguments*!

If, up until now, you have been the person in the home who has carried the mental load of the housework, you will be able to free up much more headspace and no longer shoulder the full responsibility of keeping track of what needs doing and when.

INCENTIVISING THE CHILDREN TO HELP

I believe that children need to learn how to run a home. I know that life doesn't revolve around housework, but I also know (as we all do) that it is a part of life: housework is necessary. This is why I think it is vital that young people learn how to do it as efficiently as possible. I motivate and incentivise myself to get the housework done daily by telling myself that once it is done I can forget about it and carry on with the rest of my day. This is enough for me (that and the fact that I like living in a clean house). But how do we encourage young people. Do we pay them? Do we reward them in some way?

Of course, this is down to each individual family. Only you will know what makes your kids tick and how you will be able to get them enthused about helping out. Personally, I don't financially reward my kids for doing housework. This is because I want my kids to want to help. I want them to feel the benefit of working as a team, and I want them to do this willingly, not because they have been paid £1 to empty the dishwasher.

You might disagree, though, and that is fine. Whatever works for you is the right thing to do.

My kids have grown up knowing that they are expected to help. Of course, the grown-ups still do the bulk of the housework, but even the little things that the kids do have a big impact on my and my husband's workload and they know that by pulling their weight they are helping their parents. This makes *them* feel good, and it reduces our workload, which makes me feel good. It is a win-win situation.

When everyone knows where they stand, it cuts down on the cajoling and the bribing, and it makes for a much calmer household. I only have to scroll through the comments on the TeamTOMM Facebook group to see that if housework were to be taken out of the equation, loads of couples and families would be having much fewer arguments. There is a lot to be said for encouraging children to see it as part of life early on. Because when they grow up and enter a living arrangement with another adult, housework won't be something they fight over.

If you choose to not give your kids money for doing the housework, what other ways can you use to incentivise them?

- Why not get them to help you have a big declutter and then allow them to keep the money from any items that can be sold on selling sites or at a car boot sale? Not only will this get them cleaning, but it will also nurture their entrepreneurial spirit.
- Tell them that if they help you, you will have less housework to do and this means you can all do more nice things together.
- Make it fun. There are daily cleaning playlists on Spotify (search theorganisedmum). I get so many videos of parents and their kids cleaning, dancing and having a good giggle. This type of thing is gold to kids. Spending quality time with you (even if it is cleaning) means the world to them.

WHAT EXACTLY DO MY CHILDREN DO?

Tom and Jonny are 12 and 9 at the time of writing this book, and on a daily basis they:

- Make their beds (TeamTOMM-trainee style – see page 102)
- Make their own breakfasts
- Empty the dishwasher
- Set the table
- Clear the table
- Keep their rooms tidy

Ben, who is three, at the time of writing this book:

- Tidies his toys after he uses them
- Helps to set the table/clear the table

If you are at a loss and need a little inspiration for jobs that are age appropriate, below is a handy chart to help you.

BE PATIENT

If you really want your children to help in the home and learn new skills, you are going to have to make your peace with the fact that they will need the space and the time to learn. This means coming to terms with the fact that unless you are extremely lucky, they won't do the job perfectly first time

JOBS YOUR KIDS CAN HELP WITH

Three to five years

- Put toys away

- Straighten the bed in the morning

- Put clothes in the washing basket

- Clear the table

- Lay the table

- Put away shoes/bags/coat

Five to ten years

- Strip the bed

- Vacuum

- Dust

- Make their own packed lunch (at 10 years)

- Empty the dishwasher

Ten years plus

- Change their bedding

- Take out the bins

- Do a load of laundry

- Iron their uniform

- Prepare a simple meal

- Load the dishwasher

and it will no doubt take a little bit of practice (and a lot of patience from you).

Please, please, please resist the urge to go behind them and redo their hard work, because it will knock their confidence and undermine their efforts. If imperfection in the house bothers you, practise taking a deep breath and know that in the long term the short-term pain of seeing a bed not made to your standards will pay off. Keep your eyes on the prize. I promise you that it will be worth it. Remember that we are playing the long game here. That being said, there is a technique that I have taught my older two that means that bed-making is easier for them and also much less painful for me to have to watch.

MAKING THE BED TEAMTOMM-TRAINEE STYLE

It is super-easy to make the bed this way and it can be done in about 30 seconds flat. It is much less complicated than making a bed properly and it will also allow the bed to air throughout the day (so it's perfect for the teen bedroom).

I ask my children to fold the duvet back in half over itself, straighten the bottom sheet and plump the pillows. And that is it. It looks much neater than an unmade bed, you don't have to do it and it gets them into the habit of making their beds daily. What's not to love?

9

How to Find That 30 minutes in Your Day

Many of you will probably be thinking that it's impossible to find 30 minutes per day for housework, but I want you to take a deep breath. I can help you find the time. There are 1,440 minutes in every day and I am asking you to give me 30 of them. It doesn't matter when you do these 30 minutes, or even whether you do them all in one go. What matters is that you find a way to shoehorn them into your day somehow – whether that's by managing your day more efficiently, thinking ahead and getting organised, or adjusting your morning or evening routine.

It is important because the only way for TOMM to work is if you actually do the 30 minutes each day. For things like this to work you have to use them, and this means finding the time to do TOMM and commit to giving it your best shot. I know how easy it can be to make excuses and tell yourself that you will start something fresh on Monday, but the fact of the matter is that housework won't go away if you ignore it. It will continue to build up and up until it is so overwhelming that it can't be ignored any more and you can write your name in the dust.

I can't wave a magic wand across all the homes in the world and make them magically tidy (sadly, I never attended Hogwarts), but I can show you some sneaky ways to find time that you didn't think you had.

HERE'S HOW TO FIND THE TIME

The simplest way to find extra time in your day is to master the annoying little chunks of time that you don't think you can do anything with. When these little bits get added together, they can make a massive difference. Here's what I mean:

- Do you sit through the adverts when you watch TV at night? Instead, use these two to three minutes to get something useful done, like loading the dishwasher or putting away some washing.
- Do you sit staring blankly at the bathroom wall wondering how many times you can sing 'Row Row the Boat' before losing the plot when your kids are in the bath? Stop! Take the bathroom cleaner in there and give the bathroom a quick clean while they're playing in the bubbles (obviously this is for kids who are able to sit up unaided, you should never leave children alone in the bath). You can still sing if you want to, but you will also be multi-tasking.

- While you are in the shower, how about giving it a clean while you are waiting for your conditioner to work its magic?
- Do you constantly check your phone? It is really easy to pick up your phone and lose a good chunk of your day without having actually achieved anything. How many times have you picked up your phone to check the time, only to put it down again a few minutes later and still not know what the time is?
- How often do you pop to the shops? Not only is popping to the corner shop usually more expensive than a trip to a larger supermarket, but it is also time-consuming and painful, especially if you have a buggy, your toddler and a tired child that you have just collected from school. Do your grocery shopping online. This will shave so much time off your day, especially if you are the sort of person who goes to the shops every night on the way home from the school. It will also save you battling the queues with a gaggle of kids in tow.

Meal planning

As an extension to doing your grocery shopping online, menu planning is a time-saving no-brainer. If you are usually found staring aimlessly at the shelves hoping that inspiration for tonight's meal will hit you, you will be shocked to see how much time (and money) you can save if you plan your meals (see Chapter 15 for more on this).

If you haven't already got one, I urge you to invest in a slow cooker (see Chapter 13). These are an absolute game changer, because they will eliminate the need to meal prep in the evening. At first this might seem like you are just moving meal prep from the night to the morning, a bit like borrowing from Peter to pay Paul, but the beauty of the slow cooker is that you can just quickly chop the ingredients and throw them in the slow cooker. And that can take just a couple of minutes. Most of the recipes in the food section of this book take little or no time to prepare. Take a look at the 30-second section starting on page 188.

THINKING AHEAD – BEING YOUR 'FUTURE FRIEND'

'For every minute spent in organising, an hour is earned', so said Benjamin Franklin. And it's true. How many times have you been running around in the morning, terrified that you are going to be late for work because you can't find your car keys? Things like this will eat away at your time (and sanity) and make you a massive ball of stress. Have a look at areas of your life where you can be your future friend. Being organised will save you time in the future and help you to find that extra 30 minutes in your day to follow TOMM.

The phrase 'future friend' has earned itself quite a reputation in TeamTOMM. People all over the world are being their future bestie and making their future lives easier. It might seem like a bit of a weird-and-wacky concept at first, but I promise you that it works. It is so effective that it works in almost all aspects of life. You can apply it to your job, your diet and fitness regime and your finances; basically, it is another way of saying: 'Don't put off until tomorrow what you can do today.'

The idea is that whenever you don't want to do something, you ask yourself, 'Will this make my life harder in the future? Am I being my future friend?' That future might be in an hour's time, it might be tomorrow or it might be in a few months when you are unwinding the beautifully stored Christmas lights from last December. If the answer is yes, that your life is going to be made worse in the long run by not doing something now, and there is nothing stopping you from getting it done (apart from, perhaps, the sheer lack of motivation), suck it up, be your future friend, and get it ticked off the list.

Promise me you will try it, because I guarantee you'll be muttering this little phrase to yourself in all sorts of situations, and you'll be like the cat that got the cream because you've looked after your future self.

Let's set out a scenario

It's 9pm on a Sunday night and you've left the dishes from dinner because you had eaten far too many Yorkshire puddings and wanted to watch TV instead. There's nothing wrong with that, but here's the rub. You now have two options:

1   You can either get up and feel so tired and groggy after all those Yorkshire puddings that you will not want to do the dishes, so you shut the kitchen door and go to bed.

2   You fight the urge to sleep and spend 15 minutes tidying before you head up the stairs to bed.

Let's say you went with option 1. This means that you will wake up (on a Monday morning) and have to deal with burnt-on, dried food before you even think about starting your week properly. Will this make you happy or sad? I bet it will make you sad. Were you your future friend last night? No! Are you a little bit annoyed with your past self? Yes probably.

Let's say you picked option 2. You wake up on Monday morning and come down to a nice clean kitchen. You can have your breakfast unhindered by the mess in the sink and you can get on with your day. Were you your future friend last night? Why, yes you were! Are you a much happier human for it? You bet!

Happiness is being your own future friend

The idea of being your future friend will change your life for the better. File paperwork as soon as you get it, so that you won't be frantically trying to find your home insurance documents when you have water pouring through your ceiling and you need to find the emergency hotline number. We have a filing cabinet hidden in our hallway cupboard which means that important documents that land on our doorstep either get actioned or filed straight away. It really is worth spending a couple of extra seconds putting things away properly to save you time in the future. This applies to lots of things. Take clothes as a really good – and obvious – example: if you put them away neatly they won't get creased and need an emergency iron at eight o'clock in the morning.

Have you ever heard the saying that procrastination is the thief of time? This is so true. So much time can be wasted thinking about doing something when the reality is that if you just get it done, you can clear it from your mental workload, leaving you with more headspace to get on with other stuff. We usually spend the most time procrastinating about the things we don't want to do. It is our brain's not-so-subtle way of avoiding doing them. Do yourself a favour and just do it.

Future friend is a really simple idea, but sometimes the simplest things are the most effective. Go forth and make your future life as good as it possibly can be. You will love yourself for it.

MASTER YOUR MORNINGS AND BOSS THE SCHOOL RUN

Is anyone here a morning person? I was never a natural morning person. I liked the idea of getting up at sunrise, doing a bit of morning yoga and sipping green tea while serenity oozed out of my every pore. But alas, I concluded that mornings were never going to be my forte. This probably had something to do with the fact that I have three children who shout loudly in the morning (they are not very Zen) and who I have to hustle hard to get out of the door by 8.30am.

One day I stumbled across a whole group of people who go to bed earlier and get up with the lark the next day. I was one of those zombie mums who used to stay awake as long as possible in order to get some me time, but I would then peel myself out of bed in the morning. I loved the idea of feeling fresher in the morning and gave it a go. I am now up at 5am on weekdays and in bed for 9pm. I have to say that it is working really well so far, and shifting my day like this means that I get loads of work done in the morning before the kids are up and when my mind is much calmer.

I am not suggesting that you do the same, but it is good to be aware that getting a head start on the day can help you find those elusive 30 minutes to follow TOMM as well as having a huge positive impact on your well-being. I know that if I start off my day on the wrong foot (perhaps by hitting the snooze button too many times), I feel as though I am in catch-up mode until I finally make it back to my bed in the evening.

By contrast, the mornings when I am able to tick a few things off the to-do list early are the ones that lead to the most productive and positive days. With this in mind, I have come up with some shortcuts to help you maximise your mornings and do the school run as calmly as possible. Basically, I am on a mission to discover the Holy Grail for all parents. It is a work in progress, but the following tips are a good start. Even getting up 30 minutes earlier can be a huge step in the right direction.

What you can do the night before (#futurefriend)

- Put a load of laundry in the washing machine. This means that when you wake up all you need to do is hit Start and by the time you are ready to leave the house it is finished and ready to be dried. A big proportion of your level 1 jobs can be done really early in the day.
- Make sure that everything is put away from the night before. This is crucial. In order to start the day calmly, you need to ensure that you are not starting on the back foot. Before you go to bed, do a quick check. No dishes left out in the kitchen; are the surfaces clear? Do as much as you can to make sure that you can start the next morning with a clean slate. I always find that a clear kitchen at the start of the day does wonders for my mood.
- Get everything ready for the next day the night before. Make sure you have clean clothes ready. If you have kids, make sure that their uniforms/book bags are sorted. Put the non-perishable items ready in lunchboxes; this means that all you need to do is make up a fresh sandwich in the morning.
- Always check on a Sunday what is coming up in your diaries the following week. This will mean that there is no nasty World Book Day surprise at the eleventh hour. (But if you do find yourself in a bit of a pickle, there's always Amazon Prime.)

On the day

- Set your alarm for 30 minutes before the chaos starts. The extra 30 minutes gives you time to have a shower and a cup of tea in peace. This is so much more useful than an extra half an hour in bed, as it means you can get some headspace before the madness starts. Once you are ready, make sure to put on a dressing gown over your clothes. This way you will be shielded from flying porridge.

- Have easy go-to breakfasts. This one is self-explanatory, but you need fuss-free food when you are up against it. Overnight oats are a really good one to try, as are boiled eggs. If you have children who don't really have much of an appetite first thing, keep some healthy options in your car for the drive to school, or in your bag if you walk.

- Put a routine in place and stick to it. Our weekday mornings are the same every. Single. Day. We all know what happens when, and it saves so much time (and angst). We have been following it for so long that we run a bit like a well-oiled machine.

- Timing is everything. I hate being late because it makes me really anxious, so this is a lifesaver for me. Work backwards (obvious, but so essential to calculate correctly). Start with the time that you need to leave the house, list all the jobs you need to do and work out how long each will take (be realistic). Now pop on another 15-minute contingency for unexpected events (like a poonami) and that is the time you need to get up. Don't expect to get up at 8am and leave unflustered at 8.30.

- Stick with it for at least two weeks. When you try to form new habits, you have to fake it until you make it. Commit to being more productive in your mornings, and soon it will start to feel like second nature.

- Be kind to yourself. You won't bounce out of bed like Tigger every single day, so don't write the whole day off as a failure because you slept in for 10 minutes. If you find yourself on the back foot one morning, reassess your priorities and knock off any easy-to-do jobs on your to-do list. That way you will be back on an even keel as quickly as possible.

- Make it as easy as you can for your kids to get ready. Think Velcro, not loads of buckles, buttons and zips. Make it easy for them to get themselves ready independently and you won't find yourself chorusing 'arms up', 'arms down', 'other foot'.

- Short-sleeve shirts are the way to go for the kids (even in the winter). It eliminates mucky cuffs that are a nightmare to clean, and it stops them getting their hands stuck in the ends of the sleeves when they are getting dressed.

- Make it a rule that the kids know there are no screens/play until after all the boring stuff is done. When they are working to this as their incentive, things will run much smoother than if you are trying to prise a child away from Mr Tumble at 8.35am. Once everyone is happy, and if you have a few minutes to spare, it means you can grab a bit of headspace before you have to leave.

MY CURRENT WEEKDAY MORNING ROUTINE

- 5am My alarm goes off and I go straight to the kitchen for my morning coffee. I sit in my dressing gown and go through my emails and work for about two hours.

- 7am I get showered and dressed.

- 7.30am If the kids are still asleep, I wake them up and get the level 1 jobs done.

- 7.45am We have breakfast

- 8am Sometimes I do my 30 minutes of housework; it all depends on the schedule for the day.

- 8.40am We leave the house for the school run.

- Don't be afraid to get the older kids helping out. If you can delegate some of your level 1 jobs to the older ones (like vacuuming and emptying the dishwasher), then do it. It will stop you from becoming overwhelmed, and it will also instil a sense of responsibility in them from an early age.

- For those days when you are really against the pump, and despite all your best efforts you seem to be wading through treacle, this sure-fire tip *never* fails. Go to school in your active wear. This means that you can get away with a bare face (that'll save you 10 minutes) and you can just pull on any old gym stuff, and to everyone else it will just look like you are about to go and smash out a quick 5km, when really you are going home to eat a bacon sarnie.

Even if you don't have children but fancy yourself as a bit of a morning person, something similar to my schedule is well worth a try. I promise it isn't as painful as it sounds. If I can do it anyone can! If you'd told me last year that I would be getting up with the lark I would never have believed you.

CONQUER THE EVENING ROUTINE

If you are a parent, there is a certain time of day that is difficult to restructure in a way that will make you more efficient. This is 5pm to 9pm, the part of the day when you slip into a parallel parenting universe, when both you and your kids turn into grumpier versions of your true selves and time passes so extremely slowly that it can be painful.

This time of the day can be fraught with tension. There is so much that you need to get done. Whether you have a young baby, older kids or even a mix of ages, the witching hour can seem relentless. Most of this is down to energy levels running low; it has been a long day and this is the home stretch until bedtime. Everybody is tired, stuff still needs to be achieved and you are all probably hungry – this does not make for a good mix. Keep this in mind: tiredness + hunger = witching-hour madness. Over the last 12 years I have come up with some sneaky tactics to minimise the pain of the witching hour and leave you with enough time and energy after your children go to bed to do your 30 minutes or be your future friend and prepare for the next day.

Here are some handy hints to help avoid the grim combination above.

The first thing that you need to do is to prepare yourself No, not as if you are going into battle (although it can feel like a battle at times), but begin thinking about unwinding. It isn't just your children who are in need of decompressing from the day. Whether you have just got in from work, picked up the kids from the childminder or are frantically counting down the seconds until your other half comes home, it is a really good idea to get into the habit of helping yourself switch down gears. Think about how you can do this. Everyone will be different, whether it is putting on some calm music or dancing around in your kitchen (for me it is listening to a gritty audio book while cooking), just do something different for yourself as you transition towards evening.

Try to keep your diary as free as possible You won't stand a chance of keeping this time of day calm if you have planned supermarket trips, or you have to complete work from earlier in the day or you need to run errands. Keep this time as kid-friendly as you can. It will pay off massively, because you won't be multi-tasking during what is already a time that is crammed full of potential hot spots.

Keep the kids calm Once you have dialled down your own stress levels, it is time to work on the kids. After a long day they might need help to switch to unwind mode, too. This is especially important for younger children who have the tendency to get over-tired. An over-tired child is much less able to control their emotions (come to think of it this applies to some adults I know, too). Why not try taking the dog out for a quick walk or let off some steam at the park?

If your kids are still at the age when they enjoy a bedtime story, consider switching things around a little bit and try having their story time earlier. If you read them a story earlier in the evening, it will mean that you will still have the patience to enjoy it, too. This way you won't be sneakily skipping pages in a rush to get it over with so that you can go and slump on the sofa to watch *Coronation Street*.

Get a slow cooker (seriously). Slow cookers have been sadly overlooked as old-fashioned kitchen gadgets that only cook stews, and this is such a shame because they totally rock. There have been many times when I have tried to cook spaghetti Bolognese with a toddler hanging off my leg, and if you have been there as well, you will know that it is not ideal. If you are too time-poor to prepare nutritious meals in the evening, it is well worth considering investing in a slow cooker. All you need to do is load it with ingredients earlier in the day and you will have a massive job ticked off the list. You can almost feel the pressure releasing from that time of the day already. (For lots of easy slow cooker recipes that won't have you chopping and measuring for ages, check out the recipe section of this book. And if you only try one, then make it the Fakeaway Doner Kebab on page 193.)

For those of you with young children, you might like to consider moving their bath time to earlier in the day. It is common for young babies to get fractious at bathtime. Try bathing them earlier, then you can still give them a nice calm bedtime routine but without the tears.

Don't let your blood sugar drop This one is so important and highlights just how easy it is for us as parents to let our needs slip to the bottom of the list. I bet you give your kids a snack after school, but do you have one too? As the early evening draws in you will be getting tired, so make sure you have a pick-me-up to keep you going. My personal hero snack is an apple cut into slices, dipped into peanut butter.

If you are not already in a routine, get into one Having a routine means that everyone (including you) will know where they stand, and this can really help to reduce your mental load because you will not have to second-guess and think on your feet. This applies to all ages of kids. When everyone knows the score, things run smoother. Our weekday evening routine is pretty much the same every day; we are creatures of habit, but it really helps to calm the jets.

HOW WE ROLL ON A SCHOOL NIGHT

Before I worked full-time this is how our evenings looked:

- **3.20pm** Pick up the younger two kids from school and walk home. Parking near our school (as with most schools) is a nightmare, so it means I did most of my 10k daily steps just on the school run.

- **3.45pm** All coats and bags hung up, lunchboxes washed out, remembering to put the ice pack back in the freezer for tomorrow. Usually around this time my eldest comes back from secondary school and raids the kitchen for sustenance.

- **4pm** Out of school uniforms and into the shower. Uniforms are either put into the washing machine on a quick wash or, if they can live to see another day, they are hung up. The kids shower this early for two reasons:

    1. The uniforms stay clean.
    2. It helps the kids transition from school to home.

- **4.30pm** Snack time and 30-minute screen time. If I hadn't done my 30 minutes yet, I would use this time when they are all chilling after school to get it done.

- **5pm** Homework time. How long they spend on this will obviously depend on what they have to do. If I hadn't done a workout yet, sometimes I would use this time to sneak in a bit of exercise. If I did this I would get into my gym gear before doing my 30 minutes housework and then go straight from

▶

that to a workout. This means it doesn't matter if I got hot and sweaty while I was cleaning because I was going to go straight to sweating while I exercised. I liked to call this my power hour.

Now that I am working full-time, our weekday evenings look like this:

- **5.30/6pm** I stop work and give the childminder a high five! If I haven't already done my 30 minutes, I will do them now. I also put the uniforms in for a quick wash if they need it and wash the lunchboxes.

- **6.30pm** If dinner isn't already in the slow cooker, I will start prepping dinner.

- **7pm** We all sit down to dinner.

- **7.30pm** We clear up after dinner and one of us gets the youngest ready for bed.

Homework is a particular flashpoint in the after-school cauldron. It is vital that you encourage your children to do their homework as early as possible. There is nothing worse than a whining child trying to do maths. Do it early and if they need your help you will be much better able to assist because you won't be half asleep.

If you have a small baby

Be kind to yourself. This of course applies to everyone, but if you have a colicky baby, this part of the day can be extremely challenging (I feel your pain). At this point it is important to remember that this won't last forever, the phase will pass. Carrying your baby around in a sling might help at this time of the day, but while you are going through this phase it might be wise to not attempt to achieve very much at all. Don't put yourself under unnecessary pressure.

Find some you time

Make sure that you have something grown-up to look forward to. Have things planned for later in the evening to spur you on. Get out of the house if you can, go for a walk, watch a good film, go to the gym or get a good book and snuggle down into bed as early as you can. And if all else fails, you will need wine/chocolate/Pringles and the cast-iron grit to try again tomorrow.

It is important to remember that sometimes, despite our best efforts, things don't run smoothly. Life likes to throw a spanner in the works from time to time. When things happen that are out of our control, the only thing we can do is take a deep breath and try to make the best of the situation. Whether your washing machine has broken down or you're feeling under the weather, always know that as long as you are doing your best then that is all you can do. Good enough is good enough.

WHAT DO YOU ACTUALLY DO ALL DAY?

I know how hard the motivation to stay on track with TOMM can be to cling on to when it seems that you're spending your day on a hamster's wheel full of thankless tasks. This is especially true if you feel that you are working really hard but not actually achieving very much, and it can be very much the state of play when you have small children at home with you in the day.

If you feel like this, try to document all the things that actually get done in a day. I bet it is a lot more than you think. A really lovely way of doing this was suggested to me once: get a packet of Post-it notes and every time you do a task write it on the note and stick it to your fridge. I bet that by the time you get to bedtime your fridge will be covered in Post-its and you will realise how much you have actually accomplished in your day. Even if it is 100 nappy changes.

If you work from home and are therefore constantly confronted by the housework, motivation can be a tricky one, particularly because your list of jobs can seem never-ending. When you find yourself in this situation it can be hard to stop. This is why it is important to set yourself small goals and allow yourself to feel a sense of achievement as you tick each one off. It will help to keep you motivated and in a positive frame of mind.

I work from home, and I have to be very strict with myself about my timings. I love my job and I will quite happily work away until the wee hours. This is not good for my health in the long term, and it also means that I never get a break, so I always try to structure my day into very definite segments.

- Work.
- Household duties and the cleaning. I try to do a little bit before and after work.
- Family time.
- Me time.

Everyone approaches the housework and the way they run their home differently. Some people might need help reining it in because they might be cleaning too much, whereas others face specific challenges when it comes to keeping on top of their home, whether that is working long shifts, trying to juggle it all as a single parent or just finding the motivation to get it done. I hope this chapter has given you some inspiration about how you can make TOMM work for you and your lifestyle. TOMM is hugely adaptable and has worked for me over the years despite my personal situation changing as the years have gone by. It has worked for me as a single working mum, a stay-at-home mum, running my own business (which saw me pulling 12-hour days) and as a doula on 24-hour call. In fact, it has been one of the only things that has remained constant over the last 12 years. In many ways it has been a rock that has always provided stability in my life, and I hope that it helps you in the same way.

SARAH'S STORY

I am a busy full-time mum with four children

I live with my partner, my three boys (a 16-year-old, a 14-year-old with Asperger's and a 7-year-old), my 2-year-old girl, two cats and a dog, so we have a houseful!

Most days I get up earlier than the children, so I have a bit of peace and I'm able to put the kettle on. I then unload the dishwasher, prepare the packed lunches and wake up the tribe. Next it's breakfast and getting the kids ready for school. When I come back from the school run I tend to do my level 1 jobs, then tackle whichever room it is that day. I know that if I have appointments or plans, TOMM is flexible. I normally fit TOMM in all in one go but if any of us are not well I know I can break it down and still achieve most of the housework. The system is flexible, which is realistic when you have a family.

I now have time to play with my little one in the afternoon, read or have a Netflix binge! After school we have dinner and help the kids with their homework. I have learnt to be my future friend by cleaning up the kitchen before bed and folding the washing as it comes out the dryer.

The whole house is running more smoothly. Before following TeamTOMM it was chaos. I would flit round all day feeling like I was in *Groundhog Day*, doing lots but not really achieving anything. Since following TOMM everything is so much better. It helps with my anxiety and depression. If I need motivation I watch Gemma's

Instagram stories, go to the Facebook group and put the playlist on. My laundry is always done. The basket isn't always empty but I am on top of it. I do have days when I can't be bothered but they are few and far between these days.

The plan works. It really does. Follow it, do what you can and don't worry if you don't get it all done – just prioritise those jobs the next week. Oh, and enjoy the housework-free weekends.

PART 3

Troubleshooting – How to Stay On Track

10

CBA Days

Even with the best intentions in the world, there will inevitably be times when you are not following TOMM quite as well as you'd like to be. This could be down to illness, a busy schedule, kids or a combination of all three. Nobody lives in a perfect world and life does like to throw a spanner in the works from time to time. These are the CBA days – the can't-be-ars*d days, or if you want to be polite, the can't-be-bothered days. If this happens, here is how to straighten your cap and get back on the TeamTOMM train.

I CAN'T BE BOTHERED! I'M ILL! I'M TOO TIRED!

One of the most common questions that I get asked is if I really keep up with TOMM every day. The truthful answer to that is yes, mainly because I am always trying to be my future friend (as explained in the last chapter), and by doing this I can make tomorrow as easy for myself as possible. I know that if I don't do my 30 minutes of household chores, it will still have to be done, and tomorrow I will have an hour's worth of cleaning to do. If I am just being lazy and there is not a good enough reason why I can't be doing the housework today, I'll make myself suck it up, put on some cracking tunes and just power through. Also, because I have been following TOMM for years, most of my level 2 jobs get done in less than 30 minutes, so I use this to spur me into action. One of my biggest motivators for keeping at the method is seeing how easy and quickly keeping the house clean is when you are tackling it on a daily basis. It really is the case that a stitch in time saves nine. Dust and grime build up, they are not static, and the longer they are left the worst they will become. I know that if I do not tackle it in a timely manner, I will be cursing myself under my breath when it takes longer later.

Inevitably, though, there will be days when I'm ill, the kids are ill or work gets in the way and life is hell bent on putting a spanner in the works. If you have flicked to this page because you are having one of those days today, first of all *don't panic*. Your whole house isn't going to fall apart just because you miss 30 minutes of cleaning. That is the beauty of TOMM. The method is a cumulative process, and each day builds and improves on the day before. This means that the longer you follow along, the easier it will be to keep on top of the housework. One small blip isn't going to undo all your hard work.

When those days hit, however, and believe me they will come, here is a little section to help you traverse the days when your motivation has left the building. The trick is not to let these days become the norm.

THE CBA-DAY EMERGENCY PROTOCOL

The first thing you need to do is assess why you can't be bothered. Always start here. If you have had a bad night with the baby and it feels as though you need matchsticks to keep your eyes open, the most important thing you need to do, apart from coffee, is to split up your time. Take that 30 minutes and divide it into smaller bite-sized chunks. Think 10 minutes at a time and start there. Don't think of it as a solid overwhelming wall of 30 minutes that you have to climb over – just tackle 10 minutes first. If, after the 10 minutes, you are truly exhausted, at least you have done 10 minutes – that is much better than nothing. If you feel like doing a bit more, you have two choices:

1 Power through and do the remaining 20 minutes.
2 Split the remaining 20 minutes into another two chunks and spread them over the day.

If you have had one too many CBA days of late, you might be faced with a massive mountain to climb, and this is one of the worst things to kill motivation dead. This is when the curse of 'I'll start tomorrow' or, even worse, 'I'll start Monday' can strike. The longer you leave it the worse it will become. This is fact.

If you have let the housework slide recently and you know that 30 minutes isn't really going to come close to the amount of stuff you have to do, you are a perfect recruit for the Boot Camp and you can sign up for that at the beginning of the book (see page 34). You might find that over the course of your TOMM career you have a few Boot Camps or even mini Boot Camps. I know I have, it is the reset button that is your safety net should you ever need it.

Naturally, there will be days when you just can't face lifting up the duster, perhaps you are ill or perhaps one of the kids has been ill and you have been sitting up with them all night, and the thought of doing anything other than binge-watching box sets on TV all day is just too much to bear. If this is you today, it is OK to allow yourself a day off. When these days come calling, you need to ask for extra help from those around you. If that isn't easy, for example if you're a single parent, it is totally OK to hit the pause button and leave the cleaning for another day.

Remember, it is OK to take some time out. (And you should not feel guilty about it.) If you really look deep down inside and you ask yourself, 'Do I really need to take a day off?', and the answer is yes, you need to listen to your inner voice (it is right 99 per cent of the time) and write today off. Let go of perfect, move on, and watch as much rubbish as you want on TV, have a nap, have a bath. Do whatever you need to do to refresh, and then pick up again tomorrow, guilt-free and fully charged.

Please don't think that you've failed because you have missed a day, I have a strategy coming right up in the next chapter that is going to help you catch up as painlessly as possible.

LUCY'S STORY

I am a single parent and I work shifts

I'm a 30-year-old single mum and I work shifts in the NHS. I suffer from rheumatoid arthritis and fibromyalgia, which means that sometimes I struggle to keep on top of the housework.

Since becoming a single parent five years ago, I have been at war with my house and really struggling to keep all the plates spinning. I heard about TOMM a few months back and I have been watching Gemma and learning the method. As a shift worker my rostered days vary from week to week, but I work three days between Monday and Sunday. I plan my TOMM routine depending on my shifts. I will do a maximum of two rooms on each day that I am off work (on top of my level 1 jobs). This helps me to keep up with the routine but also means that I don't spend the whole of my days off cleaning. This allows me to keep up with single-mum life and run errands – and maybe even have a cup of tea in peace, too!

TOMM has already totally changed my life. I used to go deep and hard with the housework all at once, get too overwhelmed and end up in a flare. Now I manage a set task list and the day-to-day stuff and I have *free time* on my hands to rest and recuperate between work and mum duties. It really has made such a huge difference. Thank you TOMM.

My top tips for newbies are firstly don't punish yourself if your day doesn't go to plan and you can't finish all the tasks. Life is unpredictable and loves to throw a spanner in the works. It's not the end of the world and TOMM is so easy to pick up again the following day. Also, follow Gemma's playlist. Turn it up and make it fun rather than a chore! Music is hugely motivational for me.

11

Emergency Procedures for Unexpected Guests

Urghh! Don't you just hate it when you get unexpected guests? And every single time it happens to me, I'm in my pyjamas. Even with your best intentions, and even if you have been following TOMM for a while, there will inevitably be times when your house is a little less than perfect. This is called real life, but right on cue someone will announce that they are calling in and you need a quick-fire clean-up plan asap. Fear not. Try these quick fixes to make your house appear much cleaner than it actually is.

HOW TO CATCH UP – QUICKLY

Believe it or not, you can make it seem as if you have cleaned all day when you have missed a day or two of your cleaning routine. My sneaky tricks are useful for those days when perhaps you've sat unable to move from the sofa with a cluster-feeding baby or you just can't be bothered to clean but you still need to give the impression that you have.

I was looking at my Facebook memories the other day and I saw this status from when I was still in the newborn phase with Jonny: 'A spray of polish and some bleach down the loo, and to the unsuspecting it seems like you've been cleaning all day.'

I know that some of you are convinced that I live in a palace of clean 24 hours a day, 7 days a week, 365 days a year. I hate to burst your bubble, but some days the kids get sick, or work takes over and I find myself in damage-limitation mode. I do always try to do my level 1 jobs on days like this, but I have a few quick-fix tricks up my sleeve for those days when I want to take it slightly easy but still give the illusion that I've been cleaning:

- Always open the windows. On catch-up days the first thing I do is to make sure that the house gets a really good airing. It is the best way to keep your home smelling fresh (even in the winter).
- On catch-up days it might be the case that you come downstairs in the morning and you are faced with a bit of a disaster zone. If this applies to you, take a deep breath and choose one corner of the room and start there, moving around the room clockwise, in the same way that I have described previously. Tackle everything in your path and do not deviate from the route.

- Put on your favourite tune and for the duration of this one song get rid of as much of the general clutter as you can. Concentrate on getting surfaces as clutter-free as possible. If you have other family members around at the time, the more people you can get on board with this the better.
- Depending on which days you have missed, you might be able to split the tasks across the remaining days of the week. You don't have to do the full 30 minutes, just choose the most urgent jobs from the rooms you have missed and do as much as you can for 15 minutes. This will make it much easier to add it on to the current day's jobs.
- Think about where the Friday Focus is for that week, and if it is in the room that you have missed, or if it is the miscellaneous room week, you are in luck and the cleaning gods have smiled upon you. TOMM will have you covered without you even really having to try.
- Don't panic! If your home has gone majorly astray and isn't looking its best, you can do a mini Boot Camp and reset (see page 34). I have done lots of mini Boot Camps over the years and I always feel so much better after them as I am back on a level playing field and not playing constant catch-up.

WHAT'S THAT SMELL?

Even the cleanest of houses can smell a little bit suspect. Have you ever walked into your home after a day at work and taken a sniff only to be left feeling a bit miffed because everything smells slightly stale? The chances are that your home smells less than fresh because the house has been locked up all day, and this means that the fresh air won't have been able to circulate. Here are some simple steps that you can take in order to make sure that your home stays smelling fresh for longer.

Let in the fresh air I know I've said it many times but one of the most important things that you can do to make sure that your home smells clean, as well as actually cleaning it, is by allowing the fresh air in. If you have been hanging around my social media recently you will know that I always talk about airing the rooms in the morning. Airing your home, especially in the winter, is a vital part of keeping it smelling at its best. One of the easiest ways to remember to do this is to fling open all the windows while you are getting ready in the morning. Even if you only do it for 20 minutes or so, it will make a massive difference to the way your home feels and smells.

Cooking smells are a major contributor to lingering odours, and this is why it is always important to use the extractor fan in your kitchen. It was put there for a reason, so make sure you use it. Make sure that you also clean the extractor fan filters regularly because the filters will trap grease and this will build up and eventually start to let off a stale greasy smell.

A classic mistake that people make when they are trying to make their home smell better is to try to mask the smells by using air fresheners. Although this might seem like a really good idea at the time, what can often happen is that they just cover up the nasty whiffs, leaving you with a not very nice combination of an artificially smelling air freshener with an undertone of Labrador, which is a combination of smells that I don't think is going to catch on. If you are looking for a more effective way to add a fragrance to your home, why not try using your favourite essential oil? Have fun trying out new ones and buy yourself an essential oil diffuser. Not only are they a natural alternative to synthetic products, but also I much prefer the fragrance they give off.

Talking of dogs and pets in general, for that matter, if the source of the whiff is your friendly pooch or pet, you need to deal with the source. Make sure that you groom your pet regularly and wash their bedding. I wash my dog's bedding weekly on a hot wash, but if they are prone to rolling in mud and wiping this all over their bedding, you might need to do this more often.

Do you wash your pet bowls often enough? Pet food that has solidified and dried onto the bowl can really let off a nasty smell. If your pet doesn't eat all their food, get rid of it after each feed. This will stop it smelling and also stop is attracting flies in the summer.

Make sure you clean your vacuum filter regularly, this is especially important if you have pets (our furry friends have a lot to answer for). Do you notice that when you vacuum the machine lets off a dodgy whiff? The chances are it needs a good clean. I clean the filters on my handheld vacuum cleaner every month. But always make sure that your filters are fully dry before you put them back in your vacuum.

Bin cleaning is also another great way to make sure that you are keeping nasty smells at bay. Put some old newspaper at the bottom of your bin to soak up any liquids that might seep out of the bag and into the bin. This will make it much easier to clean and much less likely to smell. If you are throwing away food items that might let off a stench (a chicken carcass or fish, for example), wrap them really well in paper before you put them in the bin and it will stop the smells from travelling into the air every time you open your bin.

Bicarbonate of soda has multiple super-powers when it comes to keeping your home smelling fresh, so make sure you always have some handy. If your carpet smells a bit suspect, sprinkle some bicarbonate of soda on it and leave to work for about 30 minutes, then vacuum it up.

Make sure to keep your dishwasher and washing machine open slightly in between uses so that they don't start to smell a little bit funky.

12

Laundry – How to Lighten the Load

One of the most common problems that people bring to me is laundry. It is a formidable beast, and it seems to be winning the battle in homes all over the world. Some people have thought up complicated systems to keep it all in check, whereas others just wear all their clothes and then, when they have run out, have a frantic laundry-filled weekend so that they don't have to go to work naked.

You only have to spend some time scrolling through the TeamTOMM Facebook group to see that many people are in search of a magic solution for laundry. If I am brutally honest, I hate doing laundry. I see it is as a pretty thankless task: the sorting, folding and putting away, not to mention the small child rolling around in paint at school with no regard for the weeping person at home who needs to get the stains out. And don't get me started on the ironing.

KEEPING ON TOP OF CLOTHES WASHING

The Holy Grail of laundry is, of course, having an empty washing basket, but that moment is always far too rare. As quickly as you empty it, it fills up again. I do know, however, that there are quite a few of you who rather like laundry and that you find it therapeutic – to you I take off my hat. But for the rest of us, here is what I do to make it all a little bit less painful.

I do a load of washing every single day. This keeps the wolf from the door and means that I can stay on top of the washing pile without it seeming like a mountain that I have to climb once a week. The laundry is part of the level 1 tasks, so this is your gentle daily nudge from me to get it done. I put my washing machine on first thing in the morning, which means that the laundry has the whole day to dry and then can be put away later on.

I also guard the washing basket like a bad-tempered Rottweiler. Nothing is getting into that basket that shouldn't be there. I try my best to make sure that only clothes that are truly dirty are allowed in. Let me explain: my kids can be slippery characters and they have worked out that it takes far less effort to put their clothes in the washing basket than it does to put them away properly. Basically, they can't be bothered to fold or hang their clothes up, so they just chuck them onto the pile. Sometimes, even if they have only been worn for a couple of hours. I know that lots of other kids do this (and some adults, too), because TeamTOMM have told me.

Don't start a new load of washing until the previous load is finished (unless you can commit to putting it all away on the same day). This is crucial. You might start off all fresh, sprightly and determined to get your washing pile down, but come five o'clock, when you are on the third load of folding and putting away, you might be more inclined to leave it and have a bath instead. This is how the piles start, and we all know how painful piles are. Remember: one at a time, little and often.

If you need further incentive to clean your clothes, buy a laundry detergent that smells fantastic. This might seem strange, but if your laundry smells nice when you are folding it, you might be transported somewhere else other than the domestic doldrums. (On a side note, if you see a strange woman sniffing all the washing powder in the super-market, that's probably me.)

WHAT IF YOU DON'T HAVE A TUMBLE DRYER?

I know loads of TeamTOMM members don't have tumble dryers and there are also lots of you who are trying to be kinder to the planet and cut down on your tumble-dryer usage. If you fall into either of these categories, here are my top tips to make drying the laundry much easier when you don't have an appliance to help you out or if the weather is not cooperating.

- **Put your washing on an extra spin** After it has run through its normal cycle, switch it to the spin cycle, and this will get even more water out and will cut the drying time down considerably. Always remember: extra spin for the win.

- **Try not to dry wet clothes on radiators,** as it can cause mould and mildew. If you really can't avoid this and need to dry clothes inside, it might be worth getting a dehumidifier. A dehumidifier will help to get rid of extra moisture from the air.

- **Get the clothes into the fresh air** as much possible, as they will dry faster this way. If you don't have a washing line, you can do this by putting them on a clothes airer (under a covered porch if it is raining) or by hanging clothes by an open window.

- **When using a clothes airer,** try to give the clothes as much room to 'breathe' as possible. Don't overload it. This will allow the air to circulate, helping your things to dry faster. One of the many plus sides of doing your laundry on a little-and-often basis is that you won't have as much to put on the airer at once.

- **If you have a local launderette,** consider using their dryers. You might even want to take a book (to get some child-free time).

- **If you are drying clothes on a clothes airer** or a washing line, carefully arrange the clothes so that they dry with as few creases as possible, it will take a bit of time, but it will save you so much more angst in the long run.

HOW TO HANG YOUR CLOTHES ON THE WASHING LINE

Follow these tips to keep creases in your clothes at bay.

- Hang shirts up by the hem or tail.

- T-shirts and tops should be pegged by the hem.

- Trousers, jeans and skirts should be pegged up by the waistband.

- If you want to further ensure that your clothes stay as crease-free as possible, add clothes pegs to the bottom of clothes as they hang so that they pull out any creases.

- Some clothes will dry better if you pop them on hangers when they are on the line. This is a great way to dry dresses, for example (just remember to use clothes pegs to secure the hanger to the line).

THE DREADED PART: THE IRONING

I am not shy to admit it: I hate ironing. But what do you do when you have an ever-increasing ironing pile that is growing into a small hill and will soon become a mountain? As my mum always says, prevention is much better than cure. I do as much as I can to make sure that my ironing pile is pretty much non-existent, and here's how I do it. Some of the things below might seem obvious, but they're worth reiterating, as they can make a big difference to coping with large piles of ironing.

- Using a low spin on the washing machine will help ensure your clothes stay as crease-free as possible. This is where you need to weigh up whether crease-free clothes or clothes that dry quicker are more important. Do you go for the extra spin or not? Reader, the choice is yours!

- If using a tumble dryer, don't overload it. This will give your stuff more room and make it less likely to crease.

- Take your clothes out of the tumble dryer as soon as they are dry. This is so important. If you leave your clothes in there all day, they will crease and make ironing them almost impossible. Be your future friend and don't leave those clothes languishing.

- Before you start ironing, organise your clothes into groups according to the heat setting that they will need. Start with items that need the cooler setting first. That way you can gradually increase the heat of the iron as you move through the sorted clothes and you won't be wasting time heating up and cooling down the iron.

- When buying clothes and bed linen look out for the ones that are easy-care or non-iron. This is seriously life changing and is a major factor in most of my bedding and clothing-purchasing decisions.

- Folding is your friend. Take the time to fold your clothes as soon as they are dry.

- Iron clothes while they are still slightly damp, it reduces ironing time significantly.
- If you have the space, try to have an ironing board set up all the time; it will make it so much easier to do small chunks every now and then, and you will save yourself the rigmarole of setting up an unwieldy board.

GEM'S TOP TIPS

 If you have clothes that have been left in the tumble dryer for longer than they should have been, and they have become creased, place a damp towel or flannel in the drum with the clothes and turn on the dryer. The steam will help the creases to fall out. Then remember to take the clothes out straight away.

If you have clothes that you need to dry fast and your tumble dryer didn't get the memo, place a dry towel in the drum and this will help the clothes to dry faster.

SOCKS AND LAUNDRY NETS

Odd socks: the other laundry conundrum. We all know how it goes: you are looking at three lonely odd socks, but you know that you put three pairs of socks into the washing machine and now three of them seem to have left their partners and gone AWOL.

There is always one sock that has hidden itself inside the duvet cover. One might have fallen down the back of the washing basket. One falls out of your arms as you are carry-ing the laundry to the washing machine, so it never actually makes it there in the first place. They get caught up in other clothes, fall off the washing line and get blown into oblivion (or the dog runs off with one).

I have tried many strategies to regain control over the sock situation in my house. I have bought everyone black socks. This seemed like a good idea in theory (if very boring), but it meant that my husband usually ended up with one child's black sock and one adult's black sock, which is not ideal when you have a proper grown-up job.

I have tried washing all the socks together, but the sheer hell of pairing them all back in one go is enough to turn me into a woman on the edge. I then tried keeping a basket for the odd socks, like a holding bay until they were reunited with their other halves, but the basket just became fuller and fuller. It was like the odd socks were laughing at me.

Then I found laundry bags, and it rocked my world. Let me tell you how I use them. Everyone in the house has their own net bag and, in this bag, they will deposit their own dirty socks and underwear. When the bag is full (but not too full, because the pants and socks need to be able to move about freely) they get put into the washing machine.

When they are clean, they are then put in the tumble dryer. This is another reason for them to not be packed into a tight ball, as they won't dry properly this way. When they are dry I hand each bag back to its owner and I am free from sock pairing tedium.

TWELVE YEARS OF EFFICIENT HOUSEWORK

What you have read in the book so far is everything I have learnt about housework over the last 12 years. This is how I manage to keep my home running smoothly while juggling lots of other balls at the same time (working, being a mum, a wife, a daughter, a sister and a friend). I have downloaded the contents of my brain into this book, so that you can benefit from my mistakes and experiences. In reality, you have pretty much read the contents of my mind. I hope you have enjoyed the ride so far, and also I hope that pretty soon you will be rocking the housework along with me.

I am not leaving you just yet, though, because a big part of running a home is preparing food. Every day we have to eat, and homemade meals are generally the best, nutritionally and financially, for everyone. I am adding here a section on making everyday meals quick and tasty, as well as a guide to your most relaxed Christmas. Coming up next you will find a selection of quick and delicious recipes to add to your repertoire. I hope you enjoy them.

PART 4

You Can't Clean on an Empty Stomach

13

Slow Cookers are Not Just for Making Stews

Running a home isn't just about cleaning it, especially if you have mouths to feed. Feeding your family is just as important as keeping their home clean. But, just like with the cleaning, there isn't always the time. Cooking, food shopping and meal planning all eat into those precious minutes that we could be spending with our family and friends, so in this chapter and those that follow I will look at ways to make those tasks much simpler.

SLOW COOKING MEANS FAST MEALS

When I taught myself to cook, it soon became clear that I didn't have the patience, the time or the budget to spend hours preparing complicated dishes. If you have ever spent hours lovingly preparing a meal only to see it being devoured by your loved ones in a matter of minutes while they were keeping one eye on the TV you will know how it can rankle your last nerve, especially if you have spent all day at work and poured the last of your energies into the evening meal. Add in fussy kids who don't eat much, and you have a recipe (pun intended) for frustration.

I grew up watching my mum and dad feeding hundreds of hungry people every day in our fish and chip shops, and it taught me to take pride in knowing that people are enjoying something that I have created. This is why I have included some easy-to-prepare family favourites for you to try later in the book. Most of the recipes use a slow cooker, meaning that even very busy people can enjoy a tasty home-cooked meal without the hassle.

I like to think of my slow cooker as a workhorse that never tires. It never moans or lets me down. It will happily work away while I am doing other stuff. Then, at the end of a long day, it makes sure that I am well fed and that I have minimal washing-up to do. It is worth its weight in gold.

I fell in love with slow cookers when I became a mum of two. Suddenly the evenings were becoming much more fraught, as I was trying to battle through the witching hour and I couldn't guarantee that I would have the time or the energy to prepare a decent meal at teatime.

I dug out the slow cooker that had been languishing in my cupboard for years, dusted it down and gave it a shot. My first slow cooker was a hand-me-down from my mum, and it was a sight to behold. A truly retro crockpot that was the most amazing shade of burnt orange. We had some good times, but I dropped it and broke it (along with a couple of my kitchen tiles) and we had to part company.

A SLOW COOKER CAN ADD VARIETY

Having bought a more up-to-date model, I started to experiment and found a whole new world of culinary possibilities opening up. I was used to cooking meals as quickly as possible and was getting a bit bored by stir-fries and quick pasta dishes. Although these meals definitely have their place in a busy parent's repertoire, slow cooking now meant that I could find a quick and easy way to produce some of my favourite meals without having to stand over a hob stirring for hours.

When you are time poor in the evening, it is so easy to reach for something quick and not necessarily nutritious. But if you have been your future friend earlier in the day (while you still had some fuel left in your tank), when you are on your last strand of nervous energy all you need to do is lift the lid and serve. What's not to love?

The slow cooker I have now is a 6.5 litre beast that can easily handle cooking for a family of five, and I have adapted so many recipes to work in the slow cooker. This is the true secret to successful slow cooking: you need to adapt recipes, and if you spend a little time experimenting and getting to know your own little workhorse, you will soon be cooking up family favourites in less time and with much less hassle.

I know that some of you will not be convinced. I know that when someone says 'slow cooker' you will immediately think of beef stew or chicken casserole, and, although these are amazing in the slow cooker, it can get a bit tiresome eating stews all the time. Who wants chicken casserole every night?

I have good news: slow cookers are so much more than that. Can I tempt you with a slow cooker Fakeaway Doner Kebab (page 193)? How about Sweet-and-Sour Chicken (page 194) or Lentil and Potato Korma (page 195)? Now that's what I am talking about!

In the recipe section of this book you will find lots of recipes that are not only mouth-wateringly good, but they will also melt your heart with the ease with which you can prepare them.

Picture the scene: it is 6.30pm and you are about to do bathtime, and you get a familiar sinking feeling in the pit of your stomach when you remember you still have to make tea. This won't happen if you deployed your slow cooker earlier in the day. This is a winner, especially if you have cooked the 30-Second Chicken (page 189).

SLOW COOKER KNOW-HOW

If you are new to the world of slow cookers, I have put together some top tips to make your first ever dalliance with your new best friend as pleasurable as possible. Once you have mastered your slow cooker you will be on the path to fuss-free, delicious family food.

- The most important thing is not to lift the lid. Leave it alone. Most slow cookers have a glass lid, so you can keep an eye on what you are cooking. You need to resist the temptation to open the lid, because you will let out the heat, and therefore the cooking time will need to be increased. Step away.
- Every slow cooker is slightly different, so take some time to get to know yours. The first few times you use it, take the cooking times as a guide. You don't need to be too worried about timings (I don't want you standing watching over the slow cooker all day – that kind of defeats the object). Once the food is cooked, it won't spoil if it is left for a bit longer (hence why slow cookers are awesome to use while you are out all day). Just make sure everything is cooked through before serving.
- Don't go crazy with the liquid. You will find that if you are adapting one of your usual stove-top recipes you won't need as much liquid. This is because while your food is cooking, the slow cooker retains the moisture and there is no evaporation. This is one of the biggest mistakes that people make, and they end up with watery and insipid sauces.
- If you find that you do need to add water, make sure it is boiling water so that you don't increase the cooking time.
- If you need to thicken up a sauce at the end of the cooking time, add a little cornflour (usually ½ to 1 tablespoon, depending on how thick you want it to be and how much liquid you have) to cold water to make a paste and then pour it to the slow cooker and stir it in really well.

- If you are adding dried herbs, add them at the beginning, but fresh herbs need to be added towards the end of the cooking time.

Later in this part of the book I will show you how to plan your meals and food shop in the most efficient way possible, saving you time and money. In the next chapter I will guide you through my hacks and top tips to help make cooking and feeding your family much easier.

14

Kitchen Hacks to Save You Money and Time

The food bill takes up a whopping chunk of household budgets, and it can be hard enough as it is to makes ends meet, but when you factor in having to balance the books while ensuring your family are fed nutritious food, it can be very challenging.

When I spent time as a single mum, my food budget was really tough to live on and I had to find as many ways as I could to make sure that I was as thrifty as possible. These are the tips that I learnt along the way. I hope that they help you to balance the need to save as much cash as possible with the ability to serve up delicious food that the family will love.

The first thing you need to do is start to plan your menus. This is the *key* to saving you money. Not only does it stop those last-minute dashes to the supermarket, but if you plan breakfast and lunches too, you can also make sure that you work with your leftovers for lunch. This means that you will lower food waste: you will be cooking once but eating twice, and you will save money.

Another major plus side of menu planning is that you will be able to work out the exact quantities you need. If you are cooking two chicken dishes, you can buy a bigger packet of chicken rather than two packs of two chicken breasts, and this will save you money.

Before you write your list, always check what you have in your cupboards. If you find some meat or fish lurking in the freezer, you can save valuable pennies on protein by using up what you have. Doing a quick five-minute stocktake will also stop you from buying another can of baked beans when you already have three in the cupboard left over from last week.

A great way to save pounds is by adding a couple of meat-free meals to your weekly menu plan. Embrace pulses (peas, beans and lentils). They can be used to make some very easy and tasty meals such as dahls and soups. They are also a great way to get a delicious meal on the table without breaking the bank. And if you just can't live without meat for an evening meal, pulses and lentils are an amazing tactic to have up your sleeve to bulk out a dish so that you don't have to use as much meat.

Think about portion control, this is a biggie and very import-ant. Check out the recommended portion sizes for adults and children (the NHS Eat Well Guide is a good source of reference). Are you serving portions that are too big? When I looked at our portion sizes a few years ago I realised that I was cooking (and wasting) far too much food. As soon as I began to serve the recommended meal sizes we started to save an awful lot of money and there was much less waste. This is better for your pocket and better for the planet.

Buy frozen vegetables or chop your own and freeze them. Not only does it save time and effort (as most of it is already chopped), but also you use only what you need. You can then put the rest in the freezer for next time.

If possible, shop online This way you won't get tempted with off-the-list purchases and you can keep a check on the total cost as you go along and amend if necessary. Most supermarkets now offer a delivery pass, which allows you to save money on delivery costs. When you unpack your online grocery shopping, have a look at the dates on the perishable foods, and if they have a short date that won't make it to the day you intend to cook them, freeze them. Just make sure you set a little reminder for yourself to take them out of the freezer.

If you happen to be loitering around the supermarket at mark-down time, use this as your chance to buy as much freezable protein as you can. Store it in your freezer and use as the building blocks for your meal plan the following week. If you do bag yourself some bargains, be sure to write on them when you put them in your freezer. This way you can make sure you are using up all your food in order.

'I AM A NEW COOK AND I FEEL OVERWHELMED'

If that's you, you are not alone – we all have to start some-where. I taught myself to cook because I was fed up with oven chips being the cornerstone of my diet. When you don't have kids it might be OK to be casual about cooking, but the responsibility of keeping young children well fed soon becomes a stark reality when they start weaning.

Over the years I have found some fantastic shortcuts to make cooking much less daunting. When I had my first baby 12 years ago I started to teach myself how to cook. Of course, I started with the good old faithful for feeding babies, Annabel Karmel, and I would spend a very happy couple of hours on a Sunday batch-cooking and freezing healthy meals for my toddler. I was cooking him pasta bakes, fish and cas-seroles, and it wasn't long before he was eating better than me. So I decided to cook an Annabel Karmel meal for all of us, and it started from there. This also meant that we could all eat at the same time, something that we still do today. Mealtimes are spent together (no TV on in the background) and I hope we continue to do this for as long as we can.

I cook from scratch every day apart from Friday – that is the cook's day off, and we have a takeaway or leftovers.

Simple ways to cut corners

If you are new to cooking, here are some tricks that will make your first steps into the culinary world much easier. Master these and you won't look back.

Use pre-chopped chilli/garlic/ginger These little pots are amazing because they take the pain out of chopping and crushing. Not only are they a massive timesaver, but also you can get them from most supermarkets and they last for ages.

Stop with all the chopping Try to use frozen chopped fruit and vegetables. Think onions/peppers/mushrooms, and so on – this is another huge timesaver. Check out the frozen vegetable section of the supermarket; you will be amazed at what you can find. There will be less waste too, as you will only use what you need. If you want to do it yourself then you can chop and freeze your own. This is also a great way to make sure that any vegetables that are languishing at the bottom of the your fridge won't go to waste.

Batch-cook I know that you will have heard this before, but bear with me. If you have a slow cooker, use it to batch-cook meals. There will be minimal extra effort and you will only have one bowl to wash up. You can then freeze the leftovers and have your own ready-meal waiting in the freezer for emergencies.

Invest in a good pair of kitchen scissors I use my kitchen scissors all the time. I use them to cut up meat straight from the packet into the pan; this means that I don't have to use a chopping board and it therefore saves on washing up. You can also use them to cut up food for toddlers or to cut pizzas and to cut up long bits of spaghetti, so that the kids (and me if I'm honest) find it easier to eat.

Make cleaning up easier Before you start to prepare a meal, make sure you have an empty dishwasher or a sink full of hot soapy water. That way you can tidy up as you go and make the clean-up operation much less of an ordeal.

Bag it up With clean-up still in mind, when you start to cook have a bag at the ready, so that you can put all the rubbish in there as you go along. Then you can easily transport it to the bin or recycling once you are done.

Think simple Master some super-simple recipes. Choose some recipes with only a few ingredients. Nothing is going to put you off more than having to buy lots of weird and wonderful things. Plus, if there are only a few ingredients, it will be easier to remember and you will know the recipe off by heart the next time you cook it.

15

How to Plan a Meal Like a Pro

Growing up in a fish and chip shop might sound like a kid's dream – to have your fill of chips, sausages, battered cod and chicken nuggets – but let me tell you, after a while it wears a bit thin. Even my mum and dad used to get sick of it. My mum would resent cooking again every night after she got home from cooking for hundreds of other people during the day. When you are the cook at work and then have to come home and cook again, it can get tiresome. I sometimes wonder if Jamie Oliver and Gordon Ramsay are secretly serving up egg and chips every night because they are completely cooked out.

Understandably, my mum did not want to cook from scratch every night – and who can blame her? She had been cooking since 11.30am and probably all she wanted to do was dive head first into her bed.

I grew up in a house that never planned a meal and, as a result, we wasted a lot of money on food. I remember walking around the supermarket with my mum on a Saturday

afternoon (her only day off) and she would work out what we
would eat for the next few days based on what she could see
in front of her. It wasn't efficient, and it was stressful for her.
Back in the dark days of the 1980s we didn't have supermarket online shopping, so my mum had no choice but to traipse
around the supermarket with every other parent on a Saturday.
Is that really what you want to be doing with your spare time?

ALL HAIL INTERNET SHOPPING!

I try to avoid doing my food shopping at the supermarket
now at all times. With three kids in tow it is not a pleasurable
browsing experience. In fact, it is more akin to having your
teeth pulled without anaesthetic. This is why I meal plan, and
why I do all my food shopping online.

I know that there are some of you out there who don't like
the thought of knowing five days in advance what you are
going to be eating. My dad is one of those people, and he
likes to live spontaneously and let his taste buds guide him on
the day. But, for many of us, our time and budgets mean that
forward planning is not only important but essential.

We all love knowing what we are having for tea at night
because it means we can be savvier with our lunch choices
and avoid eating the same thing twice in one day.

It might seem like a bit of a stretch to sit down and plan
your meals and then shop online, but when you compare this
to the time you could waste schlepping around the shops, I bet
you will soon come around to my way of thinking.

After I taught myself to cook, sitting down and planning our meals turned into a real pleasure, and I would get excited about the new meals that I would be cooking over the next few days. I meal plan every week now, and we work on a week-by-week basis. I know there are some people who like to plan for the whole month, but this has never been my preferred way of doing things. However long your meal planning is for, the following tips will help you plan like a pro. If you are one of those people who always buys a few bags of fresh herbs because you think you should, but they end up being thrown away when they turn into a mushy liquefied mess in your fridge, these tips are for you.

The first thing I do before I even sit down with a pen is to check what I already have in my freezer, pantry cupboards and fridge. Start here and find out what needs using up, and use these as your foundations for next week's meals. I will always look at protein, carbs and vegetables and see what I can make up from what I already have. If you have a slow cooker, using up stuff becomes really easy, because you can make up casseroles on the fly, and because slow cookers are so forgiving you can easily go a little bit off-piste and save yourself cash. If you haven't already tried it, I wholeheartedly recommend my Something from Nothing Tart (page 181), which is a little warrior when it comes to using up any saddened vegetables that are languishing at the back of your fridge.

Next, look at your diary and work out who is going to be home for the meals. Does Jonny have karate? Is Mike working late? Planning your meals around the activities that the family already have booked in for the week will mean that you are not staring down the barrel of cooking a complicated meal when you have only 30 minutes in between coming home from work and getting out to karate. Think about what time you will have available to prep, and plan your meals accordingly. This is where your slow cooker can really start to earn its keep.

Now you can start to think about your plan. I like to keep things as varied as possible through the week and make sure that we have a balance of vegetarian, meat and fish dishes. It just helps to keep our diets as varied as possible, and makes mealtimes interesting. Have a bird's eye view of what you will be eating over the week and try to make it as balanced as possible. Have a look to see if there is good variety in the meals that you are cooking. Are you varying your protein sources? Is there a good selection of vegetables?

Once you know what you are working with in terms of your meal needs and what you already have, head online and start your grocery order. Shopping for your food online means that you can keep a tally of what you are spending, and it is also a really quick way of searching through all the current offers. When I go online, this is where I always start. I have a look at the fresh and tinned food to see if there are any bargains that I can work into the meal plan.

Write your meal plan while you are shopping online If you sit down and write out a meal plan, and then go online, you are basically doubling the amount of time you are spending on the task, so log on, pick your meals and get them in the online basket all at the same time.

If you have a fussy eater and you are worried that they will not want to eat the same as you, and you find yourself cooking lots of different meals to cater for everyone, try to make it as fair and as inclusive as possible. I always try to make sure that there is something on the plate that a fussy eater will enjoy. And if everyone is sitting to eat at the same time, you might be surprised at the take-up of food that you would never have thought they would eat.

Make use of your favourites list Most supermarkets have a handy list of the things that you buy regularly, this takes the brain power out of stocking up on your essentials. Just remember to have a quick look in your cupboards first to make sure that you actually need them before clicking 'buy'.

Work to your budget and tweak accordingly. This is a major part of menu planning, because you can see where the majority of your food budget is going. If you have been overspending, it might be because you are buying too much expensive meat or unnecessary snacks. Meal planning will mean that the food bill is known up-front and will save you any nasty surprises, such as getting to the end of the month and realising that you have seriously overspent on food.

Make use of any leftovers for lunches the next day. If you have looked at your diary you will be able to work out if you will be at home for lunch one day, meaning you might be able to have the rest of the chicken from last night's roast dinner in a salad or a sandwich. This will save you wasting food, and it will also save you money on buying extra bits for lunches. You are in essence cooking once but eating twice.

MEAL PLAN IDEAS

To get you started, I have included four meal plans based on the recipes in this book as well as a range of ideas to feed your family at breakfast and lunch.

I hope you find some culinary inspiration within the meal plans. I know what it is like to feel as though you are eating the same meals on a repetitive cycle. Sometimes it just takes an influx of new ideas to set our taste buds alight with new and interesting meals. All the menu plans are for a family of four, but the portion sizes are generous, so if you have a toddler to feed as well (like I do), the recipes can easily stretch to fill an additional little tummy.

The pushed-for-time meal plan

These recipes will be like your knight in shining armour come the witching hour – you know, that period between four and eight o'clock when the kids seem to have been taken over by tiredness/an alien life form. Family life is busy, and teatimes can be fraught. If you are pushed for time but want to avoid serving up beans on toast every night, give this meal plan a go. All the recipes are listed in the recipe section, and some of them take only 30 seconds to prepare.

Monday	Super-Simple Salmon en Croute	(page 192)
Tuesday	30-Second Chicken	(page 189)
Wednesday	Knock-Your-Socks-off Lentil and Potato Korma	(page 195)
Thursday	Bacon-Wrapped Cod	(page 193)
Friday	Classic Spaghetti Sauce	(page 183)
Saturday	Fakeaway Slow Cooker Doner Kebab	(page 193)
Sunday	30-Second Sunday Lamb	(page 191)

The strapped-for-cash meal plan

When it seems that there are too many days at the end of the month until pay day, you will want to reach for recipes that are budget-friendly but don't taste like it. When I was a single mum, money was tight, but the cooking skills that I had learnt in the previous years stood me in good stead and helped me to produce tasty food on a very small budget.

Monday	Something from Nothing Tart	(page 181)
Tuesday	Slow Cooker Arrabiata	(page 183)
Wednesday	Cowboy Baked Beans	(page 185)
Thursday	Where've You Bean? Chilli	(page 186)
Friday	Slow Cooker Curried Cod	(page 201)
Saturday	Slow Cooker Peri Peri Chicken	(page 190)
Sunday	Slow Cooker Beef Brisket	(page 190)

The newbie-cook's meal plan

Finding your feet in the kitchen shouldn't be daunting – it should be fun. If you are new to the world of tsp (teaspoon), tbsp (tablespoon) and julienned carrots (carrots cut into matchsticks), this meal plan is a great place to start. Slow cooker meals feature heavily in this meal plan, and that is because they are so forgiving: you don't have to be watching the timer like a hawk with these meals. Relax and enjoy adding some new meals to your growing repertoire.

Monday	Slow Cooker Puttanesca Sauce with pasta	(page 184)
Tuesday	Bacon-Wrapped Cod	(page 193)
Wednesday	Sausages and mash with Cranberry Gravy	(page 205)
Thursday	Slow Cooker Chilli	(page 198)
Friday	Jonny's Chorizo Chicken	(page 199)
Saturday	Slow Cooker Meatballs	(page 198)
Sunday	Super-Simple Salmon en Croute	(page 192)

Gem's faves meal plan

This meal plan is a little bit of me. This is my idea of food heaven and features some of my favourite recipes from the book. We are guaranteed to be eating at least one meal from these faves each week in our house.

Monday	Cod with Easy Gremolata	(page 204)
Tuesday	Knock-Your-Socks-Off Lentil and	
	Potato Korma	(page 195)
Wednesday	Sweet-and-Sour Chicken	(page 194)
Thursday	Slow Cooker Curried Cod	(page 201)
Friday	Fakeaway Slow Cooker Doner	
	Kebab	(page 193)
Saturday	Red Thai Prawn Curry	(page 200)
Sunday	Slow Cooker Beef Brisket	(page 190)

BREAKFAST IDEAS

My dad always says that having breakfast is like putting petrol in your body's tank first thing in the morning and that it is vital to give your day a kick-start with some decent food. Breakfast time can be hectic, and very often it's just a piece of toast grabbed on the way out the door. If you are in a breakfast rut, sometimes all it takes to help you climb out is someone giving you some new ideas. Here are mine:

- Lightly toasted bagel topped with cream cheese and sliced strawberries (tastes like a strawberry cheesecake).
- Boiled eggs with toasted soldiers.
- Porridge with a handful of frozen fruit stirred through. Frozen blueberries are our favourite.
- Cinnamon eggy bread: whisk 3 eggs with 2 tablespoons milk and add ½ teaspoon cinnamon. Fully immerse a slice of bread into the mix and fry each side

lightly in coconut oil until they are lovely and golden. Serve with maple syrup.

- Potato patties with fried egg: take some leftover mashed potato and stir through some cooked spinach. Take a handful of the potato mix and form it into a patty. Fry over a medium heat in a little oil on each side until crispy and the potato is heated through. Serve with a fried egg.
- Peanut butter on toast topped with sliced apple. Sprinkle some cinnamon on top to make it extra special.
- Smoked salmon with poached eggs.

LUNCH IDEAS

Lunch needn't be boring but sometimes it can feel like yet another thing you have to think about in an already busy schedule. Buying lunch at work or school can also prove to be expensive. If you are looking for inspiration to help make lunch times easier, this section is for you.

For the kids

If you are sick of making the same old curled-up sandwiches every day, try these ideas to help spice up their lunchtimes. You might like to steal a couple of ideas for your work pack-up too.

Tom's Favourite Couscous Salad Soak the couscous according to the instructions on the packet. (If you are using plain couscous, add a stock cube to the water.) Once cool, toss in some roasted vegetables and sweetcorn. (Don't forget to pack a fork.) If you want to make it meatier, add some cooked chicken.

Ben's Favourite Green Goddess Pasta Ben doesn't like bread, so he doesn't eat sandwiches, which means packed lunches are a little tricky. Thank goodness for this Green Goddess Pasta that he basically inhales every time it is put in front of him.

Cook your child's favourite pasta according to the instructions on the packet and allow it to cool. Stir in some green pesto and chopped cooked broccoli. If you want you can sprinkle some cheese on top.

Jonny's Favourite Sweet Chilli Chicken Wrap Jonny loves a wrap, and I love making them for him because I know that he will wolf it down. Use chicken left over from the Slow Cooker Peri Peri Chicken to add the ultimate in lunchtime zing.

Put some leftover cooked chicken and a handful of shredded lettuce on a tortilla wrap. Squeeze on some sweet chilli sauce and roll it up. Wrap in foil to keep it all together.

Something from Nothing Tart Add a slice from the selection on page 181 to your lunch box for a tasty treat.

For the grown-ups

I see lunchtime as my little sanctuary in the middle of the day. I always try to sit down and eat my food away from my work, somewhere I can zone out and make some space for myself in the middle of a busy day. Here are some of my favourite lunches.

Warming Sweet Potato Soup (page 188). I love this soup and it is a real crowd pleaser when the weather is colder.

Toasties I bought myself a stove-top toastie maker and basically fell in love with it. I'm dairy free so I don't use butter in my toasties but feel free to go for it if you love the taste of butter.

Pizza Toastie Spread two thin slices of bread with some tomato purée on each side and add four slices of pepperoni to one slice. Sprinkle over some Cheddar cheese (I use dairy-free), then pop the other half of the sandwich on top and heat.

Tuna and Cheese Toastie Put some canned tuna on a thin slice of bread and sprinkle over some grated Cheddar cheese (I use dairy-free). Season well, then pop another thin slice of bread on top and heat.

Ham and Cranberry Toastie Put one slice of ham on a thin slice of bread and sprinkle over some Cheddar cheese (I use dairy-free). Spread some cranberry sauce over another thin slice of bread. Pop one on top of the other and heat.

Sweet Potato Wedges with a Spicy Mayo Dip Preheat the oven to 200°C (180°C fan oven), Gas 6. Toss some sweet potato chunks in olive oil or coconut oil and put them in a roasting tin. Roast for 30–40 minutes until golden. Serve with a dollop of mayonnaise with some cayenne pepper stirred through.

Prawn and Avocado Salad Make a quick dressing with a squeeze of lemon juice, a squeeze of lime juice and 1 teaspoon olive oil, and season with salt and pepper. Drizzle this over cooked prawns and chopped avocado.

Tuna Pâte on Crispbreads Put 1 small can of tuna, drained and rinsed, into a food processor and add 1 teaspoon capers, 1 small handful of tarragon, 1 small handful of basil leaves, 1 tinned anchovy, 1 tablespoon olives, 1 teaspoon Dijon mustard, the juice of ½ lemon and 1 tablespoon olive oil. Whizz until just blended. Serve with crispbreads, crackers or toast and some salad.

16

The Recipes

I love cooking, almost as I much as I love eating, and now-adays food is very important to me. I cook from scratch most of the time and take pleasure in creating food that I know my family will love.

As a family we sit down together every night at the dining-room table. We have a no-TV rule, and it is a lovely end to the day. I am very lucky that my kids are up for trying most of the meals that are put in front of them, but I would be lying if I said it was always this way. When Tom and Jonny were little we only ever had one rule at mealtimes: they had to try their meal. If they didn't like it, that was fine, but the most important thing was that they gave it a go. Even if it was the teeniest, tiniest of mouthfuls. Ben is at this stage now (he is only three) but the number of meals and foods that he enjoys is rising slowly by the week. I know it takes patience, and I know how disheartening it can be to cook a meal only for little noses to be turned up at it. For those of you with fussy eaters, my advice is to stay calm and make sure that there is at least one thing on the plate that you know they will love.

At the start of this book I told you that when I first became a mum I wasn't much of a cook, and when it came to creating family meals I was certainly challenged. You can't really feed a weaning baby a Pot Noodle, so I had to teach myself how to cook. As you can imagine, there were a few disasters and, as with any new skill, it took time and practice, but with patience I started to pick it up.

I have Annabel Karmel and Jamie Oliver to thank for easing me into the world of home cooking. My most thumbed cookbook is still Jamie's *Ministry of Food*; it has completely lost its cover and is hanging together by its binding (it is almost 13 years old, after all). I can't bear to part with it because it reminds of my first steps on the path to culinary enlightenment.

As a busy mum of three I need meals that are easy to prepare but have maximum impact on the taste buds. Sadly, it is rare that I have the time (or the energy) to stand stirring a pot for hours. I have homework to help with, a job to do and kids to look after. But I also want us all to eat well. In this chapter you will find simple, quick-to-learn recipes for you to add to your collection. They are not only easy and delicious, but also they don't require a trip to the outer reaches of the universe to track down a weird and wacky ingredient that costs the earth and will only be used once.

Because the recipes are fuss-free, it means that they are perfect if you are just dipping your toe into the world of cooking. I have never been one to sit and measure and weigh out ingredients to the exact gram (I haven't got the patience, and

I much prefer to let my taste buds guide me). This is why most of the recipes in the book are forgiving and can be prepared in little or no time at all. You can adapt and tweak them to suit you and your family's tastes. And if you are dairy-free (like me), any time that cheese or milk is called for feel free to substitute it for a dairy-free version.

Happy cooking!

CHEAP 'N' EASY MEALS

Good food doesn't have to cost the earth and nor does it have to take hours to prepare. Here are my go-to meals for when time is short and cash is tight!

SOMETHING FROM NOTHING TART

This recipe is so blooming versatile. You can pretty much put anything on top. There are lots of variations you can try. Here are my favourites, but don't be afraid to experiment. I would serve this with baked beans or roasted vegetables in the winter and a crisp salad in the summer. It also lovely cold the next day, so it's perfect to pop into a packed lunch.

Serves 4

1 roll of ready-made puff pastry

1 jar green pesto

1 handful of cherry tomatoes, cut in half

1 red pepper, deseeded and roughly sliced

1 yellow pepper, deseeded and roughly sliced

1 red onion, sliced

salt and ground black pepper

Preheat the oven to 220°C (200°C fan oven), Gas 7. Unroll the pastry on a baking tray (if it comes rolled in greaseproof paper, you can use this to line the tray). Spread the pesto evenly over the pastry. Scatter the veg over and season with salt and pepper. Bake for 20–25 minutes until the pastry is cooked and golden.

Variations

Cheat's Puffed Pizza Spread 1 tube tomato purée evenly over the top of the pastry. Scatter over some pepperoni slices and tinned or fresh pineapple chunks, then top with a handful of grated mozzarella.

Cheese and Tomato Spread 1 jar of red pesto evenly over the top of the pastry. Lay 4 large sliced tomatoes over the top and sprinkle with grated Cheddar cheese.

SLOW COOKER PASTA SAUCES AND SIMPLE DISHES

These can be used to form the base of lots of meals as well as being used on their own to serve with pasta.

CLASSIC SPAGHETTI SAUCE

Master this and the world will be your oyster. This will form the foundation for so many meals: meatballs, spaghetti Bolognese and lots of Italian-type casseroles. The beauty of this is that because you are cooking it slowly the flavour of the tomatoes will be released, and you will be left with a taste sensation.

Serves 4

2 punnets of cherry tomatoes

2 tsp Very Lazy garlic

2 tsp dried basil

2 tsp dried oregano

1 kg passata

1 tube of tomato purée

1 tbsp sugar

2 bay leaves

salt and ground black pepper

Put everything in the slow cooker, stir and cook on Low for 8 hours. Take out the bay leaves and serve with pasta of your choice. (This is great to make in advance and freeze.)

SLOW COOKER ARRABIATA

This makes a spicy tomato sauce, so if you are introducing your little ones to spice in their meals, feel free to halve the amount of chilli. This makes a lot of sauce and is great for freezing and keeping for emergency 'I forgot to do the online order' meals.

Serves 4

2 punnets of cherry tomatoes

1½ tsp Very Lazy garlic

1½ tsp Very Lazy chilli

1 tsp dried basil

1 tsp dried oregano

1 kg passata

1 tube tomato purée

1 tbsp sugar

1 tbsp chopped sun-dried tomatoes

2 bay leaves

salt and ground black pepper

Put everything in the slow cooker, stir and cook on Low for 8 hours. Take out the bay leaves and serve with pasta of your choice.

SLOW COOKER PUTTANESCA SAUCE

This is such a lovely twist on the run-of-the-mill pasta sauce and tastes amazing in the warm evenings when eaten outside. Don't let the addition of the sardines scare you – they add a lovely depth of flavour. All my kids love this, and its tastes sophisticated enough that the adults enjoy it too. It goes amazingly with a lovely glass of red while sitting on the patio.

Serves 4

2 punnets of cherry tomatoes

1½ tsp Very Lazy garlic

1½ tsp Very Lazy chilli

1 tsp dried basil

1 tsp dried oregano

1 kg passata

1 tube tomato purée

1 tbsp sugar

120g can sardines in tomato sauce, mashed with a fork

Put everything in the slow cooker, stir and cook on Low for 8 hours. Serve with pasta of your choice.

COWBOY BAKED BEANS

Who doesn't love beans on toast or beans on a jacket potato? This also goes really well with a crusty baguette and is a great choice for those busy evenings when the weather is drawing in and only comfort food will do. This makes a great side dish for sausages and is also fab as a standalone meal. Serve with veg or a crunchy salad.

Serves 4

250g chopped chorizo

1 onion, chopped, or 1 handful of frozen chopped onions

4 tbsp tomato purée

2 tbsp brown sugar

1 tsp dried sage

1 tsp Very Lazy garlic

3 × 400g cans of white beans, drained and rinsed (I use a mixture of cannellini and butter beans)

salt and ground black pepper

Put everything in the slow cooker. Add 200ml water, stir and cook on Low for 6 hours.

WHERE'VE YOU BEAN? CHILLI

This vegetable chilli is bulked out with lots of lovely beans, and this means that it feels mighty and meaty enough for meat lovers. It's perfect for when you are trying to make the cash stretch further. This is fabulous served with fluffy rice or a jacket potato and some steamed green veg. Any leftovers taste amazing reheated the next day.

Serves 4

2 onions, chopped, or 2 handfuls of frozen chopped onion

2 × 400g cans black beans, drained and rinsed

400g can kidney beans, drained and rinsed

1 kg passata

1 tube tomato purée

1 tsp Very Lazy chilli

1½ tsp Very Lazy garlic

2 tbsp black treacle

1 vegetable stock cube, crumbled

a pinch of salt

a large pinch of cayenne pepper

Put everything in the slow cooker, stir and cook on Low for 8 hours.

SOUPS

I don't always want a substantial lunch, so soups are perfect for when a lighter meal is called for. Here are a few of my faves.

PEA AND MINT SOUP

The vibrant green of this soup will please your eyes almost as much as the taste will please your tummy.

Serves 4
900g frozen peas

1 onion, chopped, or 1 handful of frozen chopped onions

2 vegetable stock cubes, crumbled

1.2 litres boiling water

salt and ground black pepper

Put everything in a saucepan, bring to the boil, then simmer over a medium heat for 20 minutes. Whizz using a blender or food processor until you get a smooth consistency. Adjust the seasoning with salt and pepper.

Variation
This also tastes lovely with a handful of watercress thrown in before you blend it.

WARMING SWEET POTATO SOUP

If you have a soup maker, this recipe is perfect. My soup maker takes 30 minutes (what a glorious coincidence), so I can whack in all the ingredients for this amazing soup and know that when I've finished my TOMM for the day it will be waiting for me as a reward. It goes perfectly with a crusty roll. Eat this while you survey your wonderfully clean home.

Serves 4

750g sweet potatoes, peeled and chopped

1 onion, roughly chopped

400ml can coconut milk

1 vegetable stock cube, crumbled

salt and ground black pepper

Put everything in a saucepan and add 100ml water, bring to the boil, then simmer over a medium heat for 30 minutes. Whizz using a blender or food processor until you get a smooth, thick consistency. Adjust the seasoning with salt and pepper.

MEALS PREPPED IN 30 SECONDS (OR THEREABOUTS)

You really couldn't get any quicker than these recipes, because they take seconds to prep. The slow cooker recipes cook all day and then you're left with a feast that looks as though you've been tending to dinner all day long. Your secret will stay safe with me.

There are also super-quick fish recipes that look and taste fantastic.

30-SECOND CHICKEN

This recipe has caused quite a stir among TOMMers – cook it once and it will be put firmly on your list of tried-and-trusted favourites. It is so versatile that you can use it for a roast dinner or to cook chicken for salads and sandwiches. If you are an avid meal prepper, you will love this, but, even better, it uses no oil, so it is healthy too. Serve with green vegetables or Roasted Cauliflower (page 204) and either mashed or roast potatoes.

Serves 4

1 whole chicken

1 lemon, cut in half

1 tsp Chinese five-spice powder

1 tsp sea salt

1–4 tsp gravy granules, according to preference (optional)

Remove any string from the chicken and the giblets, if there are any. Put the chicken in the slow cooker with the lemon halves, and sprinkle the five-spice powder and sea salt on top. Cook on Low for 8–10 hours (depending on the size of the chicken). Make sure that the chicken is cooked through before serving: test by piercing the thickest part with the point of a knife; the juices should run clear and the flesh should be white, not pink.

You will see that even though you have not added any liquid to the slow cooker, after the cooking time is up your chicken will be sitting in what will be the base for a wonderful gravy. Use gravy granules to thicken it up, if you like.

Variations
The possibilities for jazzing the chicken up are endless, but these are my faves:
Garlic Chicken Add a garlic bulb, cut in half, to the slow cooker and sprinkle 1 tsp sea salt on top.
Peri Peri Chicken Sprinkle 2 tbsp peri peri spice mix over the chicken. (This goes wonderfully with potato wedges and sweetcorn.)

SLOW COOKER BEEF BRISKET

You really can't beat this one. Serve it with Yorkshire puddings, and roast potatoes and steamed broccoli for the ultimate Sunday comfort food.

Serves 4
1kg beef brisket
100ml Worcestershire sauce
salt and ground black pepper

Remove any string from the beef brisket. Put the brisket in the slow cooker. Pour over the Worcestershire sauce and season well with salt and pepper. Cook on Low for 8–10 hours until the meat is meltingly tender.

30-SECOND SUNDAY LAMB

I always struggled with roasting the perfect leg of lamb, and for that reason I shied away from cooking it, which always made me sad, because I love lamb. Then I tried it this way and it rocked my world. Please don't let the anchovies put you off. They melt away when the lamb cooks, and they add a wonderfully deep flavour to the sauce that is left at the bottom of the slow cooker. To make this sauce into a beautiful gravy, thicken it up with gravy granules.

This is perfect for a Sunday that is full of football practices: it takes no time to prep and will give you something to look forward to while your toes are freezing on the side lines. Serve with roast potatoes and Braised Red Cabbage (page 202).

Serves 4

½ leg of lamb (about 1 kg)

1 small can of anchovy fillets, drained

1 lemon, cut in half

1 tsp dried rosemary

1–4 tsp gravy granules, according to preference (optional)

Make incisions in the lamb with a sharp knife and poke in the anchovies. Put the lamb and the lemon halves in the slow cooker and sprinkle with rosemary. Cook on Low for 9–10 hours until the meat falls away from the bone. Use gravy granules to thicken up the juices, if you like.

SUPER-SIMPLE SALMON EN CROUTE

This takes slightly longer than 30 seconds, but the speed and ease that you can make this means it definitely deserves a space in the speedy section. It is so easy that I would say it was more of an assembly job than a recipe. Serve with new potatoes and green vegetables or a big salad.

Serves 4

1 pack of ready-rolled puff pastry

4 salmon fillets (about 125g each)

1 jar of pesto

4 tomatoes, sliced

Preheat the oven to 220°C (200°C fan oven), Gas 7. Unroll the pastry on a baking tray (if it comes rolled in greaseproof paper, you can use this to line the tray). Lay the salmon fillets closely together in the centre of the pastry, making a block of four, and leaving a clear edge all around for folding the pastry over. Spread the pesto over the top of the salmon.

Pop the sliced tomatoes on top of the pesto and fold the pastry over to form a parcel. It doesn't matter if it doesn't quite meet in the middle. Trim any excess pastry off the ends and seal them together. Bake for 35 minutes or until puffed and golden. Serve in slices.

BACON-WRAPPED COD

You will have your family staring open-mouthed at your newly found culinary prowess when you serve this dish. Potato wedges and a leafy green veg go well with this, plus some garden peas that have some mint sauce stirred through.

Serves 4

4 tbsp pesto

4 skinless and boneless cod fillets (about 125g each)

8 rashers of smoked streaky bacon

Preheat the oven to 200°C (180°C fan oven), Gas 6. Spoon 1 tbsp pesto onto each cod fillet and wrap it in two pieces of bacon. Bake for 20 minutes or until the bacon is crispy and the cod is cooked through.

FAKEAWAYS

If you only try one recipe in this book, I implore you to try this kebab recipe, it will mess with your mind, because you won't believe that it was cooked in the slow cooker.

FAKEAWAY SLOW COOKER DONER KEBAB

This is by far one of the most popular recipes on my blog. It tastes just like the real thing, but it is much healthier. It is perfect for a Saturday night in front of a good film. It is perfect served with warm pitta breads, a lovely big salad and a sauce of your choice.

Serves 4

500g minced lamb

1½ tsp Very Lazy garlic

1 tsp Very Lazy chilli

2 tsp dried oregano

2 tsp dried rosemary

1 tsp salt

1 tsp ground black pepper

Put all the ingredients in a bowl and mix together really well (this is key to getting the right texture), then form the mix into a rugby-ball shape. Put into the slow cooker and cook on Low for 7 hours. Slice very thinly to serve.

SWEET-AND-SOUR CHICKEN

The kids will love the sweetness of this, and you will love the way it is so easy to make.

Serves 4

400g can of pineapple chunks

2 onions, chopped, or 2 handfuls of frozen chopped onions

2 handfuls of frozen stir-fry vegetables

3 tbsp tomato purée

50ml soy sauce

50ml balsamic vinegar

1 tsp Very Lazy ginger

1 tsp Very Lazy garlic

2 tsp Chinese five-spice powder

4 chicken breasts, chopped

225g can water chestnuts, drained

½ tbsp cornflour (optional)

Pour the juice from the can of pineapples into the bottom of the slow cooker. Put the chunks in a bowl in the fridge ready to use later. Add the remaining ingredients, except the water chestnuts and cornflour, to the slow cooker. Add 300ml water, and give it all a really good stir. Cook on Low for 8 hours.

About 30 minutes from the end of cooking, add the pineapple chunks and the water chestnuts, and pop the lid back on. If you want to thicken it up slightly, make a paste with the cornflour and a little water and stir it in 10 minutes before the end of cooking.

KNOCK-YOUR-SOCKS-OFF LENTIL AND POTATO KORMA

This vegetarian version of the classic korma is just as good as a meat version and you won't miss the meat at all. This makes a really generous portion, and any leftovers will taste amazing reheated the next day. Serve with rice and/or a selection of bright vegetables – frozen mixed veg is handy and nutritious.

Serves 4

300g korma paste

1 tsp Very Lazy ginger

1 tsp Very Lazy garlic

2 onions, chopped, or 2 handfuls of frozen chopped onions

1 tsp nigella seeds

1 tsp cardamom seeds

500g new potatoes, chopped

150g red lentils

400ml can coconut milk

2 tbsp smooth peanut butter

2 handfuls of fresh spinach

Put all the ingredients, except the spinach, into the slow cooker and add 400ml water.

Cook on Low for 8 hours. About 30 minutes from the end of cooking, add the spinach and pop the lid back on. You might want to use these 30 minutes to get your TOMM jobs done with the smell of the korma spurring you on.

FAMILY FAVOURITES

I am lucky that my older children will more or less try anything that is cooked for them. That being said, there are a few meals that are requested more often than others. Here are our tried and tested favourites.

EASY QUESADILLAS

Here is a recipe that allows you to use up food that might be going begging in the fridge. Serve it with a big salad.

Serves 4

spray oil

1 tsp Very Lazy garlic

1 red onion, sliced

4 peppers (any colour), deseeded and sliced

8 tortilla wraps

250g pack cream cheese

8 tbsp grated Cheddar cheese

Heat some spray oil in a saucepan and lightly fry the garlic, onion and the peppers over a medium heat until they start to soften and the peppers start to char slightly.

Spread each tortilla with an even layer of cream cheese, making sure to get all the way to the edges.

Divide the pepper and onion mixture among four of the tortilla wraps and sprinkle over some Cheddar cheese.

Top with the remaining wraps, cream-cheese side down, making sure to press down firmly on the edges so that the cream cheese acts as a seal.

Heat some spray oil in the frying pan over a medium heat and gently cook one tortilla at a time – don't have the heat up too high or you will burn them. When the bottom of the wrap is a lovely golden colour, turn the quesadilla over and cook the other side. The cheese will melt and be gorgeously gooey. Keep each quesadilla warm in the oven while you cook the others.

Cut into quarters using a pizza cutter and serve.

SLOW COOKER MEATBALLS

When you are pushed for time, the last thing you want to do is to start hand-rolling meatballs. It is totally OK to take short-cuts. Of course, you could take the ultimate shortcut and use a shop-bought sauce, but this way I find the flavour has much more depth. Serve with spaghetti, topped with a sprinkle of Parmesan cheese and with a salad on the side.

Serves 4

ingredients For Classic Spaghetti Sauce (page 183)

24 ready-made meatballs

Pour the sauce ingredients into the slow cooker and top with the uncooked meatballs. Stir gently so as not to break them up. Cook on Low for 8 hours.

SLOW COOKER CHILLI

I love a good chilli, and the secret to this one is the addition of black treacle – it takes the dish into a whole other level. Serve with rice or a jacket potato and some fresh veg. This is perfect Bonfire Night food.

Serves 4

1 onion, chopped, or 1 handful of frozen chopped onions

500g minced beef

1 handful of chopped mixed peppers (fresh or frozen)

1 kg passata

4 tbsp tomato purée

400g kidney beans, drained and rinsed

2 tbsp black treacle

½ tsp cayenne pepper

1 tsp Very Lazy chilli

1 tsp Very Lazy garlic

salt and ground black pepper

Put everything into the slow cooker, stir and cook on Low for 8 hours.

JONNY'S CHORIZO CHICKEN

This is Jonny's favourite meal of all time. He would happily eat it every day if he could. Serve it with crispy roast potatoes and green beans for the win.

Serves 4

225g chorizo, sliced

1 onion, chopped, or 1 handful of frozen chopped onions

1 tube tomato purée

500g passata

1½ tsp Very Lazy garlic

4 chicken breasts, chopped

100ml red wine

1 chicken stock cube, crumbled

salt and ground black pepper

Put everything in the slow cooker, stir and cook on Low for 8 hours.

RED THAI PRAWN CURRY

If there was ever a dish that was made to be eaten with a jacket potato, this is it. This is probably one of the most complicated recipes in the book, but it is so worth it. Serve with fluffy rice or a crispy baked potato.

Serves 4

spray oil

1 onion, chopped

3 tbsp red Thai curry paste from a jar, or as directed on the label

400ml can of coconut milk

fish stock cube, crumbled

2 handfuls of green beans (fresh or frozen)

2 handfuls of other veg, such as Tenderstem broccoli, baby corn,
    and so on

1 tbsp sugar

300g raw prawns, defrosted if frozen

salt and ground black pepper

Coat a heavy-based saucepan with spray oil and fry the onion over a medium heat until soft.

Add the red Thai paste (the amount you use will depend on the paste that you use, so check the instructions on the jar, I use about 3 tbsp). Turn the heat down slightly and let the paste cook for 3 minutes.

Add the coconut milk, the fish stock cube and 350ml water. Stir to combine.

Add all the veg and the sugar, and season with salt and pepper. Stir well, then bring to the boil. Reduce the heat and simmer for 30 minutes until the sauce has thickened, stirring occasionally.

Adjust the seasoning with salt and pepper, then turn up the heat and add the prawns. Give it a couple of good stirs so that the prawns have even access to the heat. Cook for 5 minutes or until the prawns are cooked through (remember: the bigger the prawns the longer they will take to be ready, so check your packet instructions).

SLOW COOKER CURRIED COD

If you want to get your kids to eat more fish, this is a great way to serve it up. The curry is lovely and warming, and it tastes great with couscous – or, as we call it, baby rice. Serve with a green veg.

Serves 4

2 × 400g cans tomatoes

2 tbsp tomato purée

400g chickpeas, drained and rinsed

1 onion, chopped, or 1 handful of frozen chopped onions

2 tbsp curry powder

1 tsp Very Lazy ginger

1 tsp Very Lazy garlic

juice of 1 lemon

4 cod fillets (about 125g each)

1 handful of fresh parsley, leaves chopped

Put everything, except the cod fillets and parsley, in the slow cooker. Stir, then cook on Low for 8 hours. An hour before the end of cooking, add the cod fillets, skin side up. Season with salt and pepper. When the cod is cooked – it will be white and will flake easily – serve with the parsley sprinkled on top.

SIDE DISHES AND ACCOMPANIMENTS

It can be hard to think up new and interesting side dishes, especially if you have children who regularly turn their noses up at vegetables. Here are some winning sides that will have them coming back for more.

BRAISED RED CABBAGE

This really couldn't be easier to make and tastes wonderful with the 30-Second Chicken on page 189 or the 30-Second Sunday Lamb (page 191).

Serves 4

1 red cabbage, sliced very thinly

2 tbsp balsamic vinegar

1 tbsp sugar

salt and ground black pepper

Put all the ingredients in a heavy-based saucepan and add 200ml water. Stir well. Cover and cook over a low heat for 2 hours, checking frequently to make sure that it isn't drying out – add a little more water if it starts to stick to the pan.

QUICK SIDES

If you are on the hunt for some super-quick dishes to serve alongside your mains, here are my top picks to have to hand for emergencies.

- Frozen mixed vegetables/peas/corn on the cobs (kids love picking them up and eating them with their hands)
- Jars or tins of pickled beetroot (great for adding to a salad)
- Grated carrot mixed with some salad dressing and a handful of raisins (makes a wonderfully sweet accompaniment)
- Mashed sweet potatoes, which provide a lovely change from regular mashed potatoes
- Tinned mixed bean salads are healthy and ready in seconds

ROASTED CAULIFLOWER

If you are trying to get your kids to eat more vegetables and they are not fans of cauliflower (perhaps you are not a huge cauliflower aficionado either), this will hopefully change your mind. Roasting cauliflower gives it a whole new dimension. It can be used as a fab side dish to the 30-Second Chicken, the 30-Second Sunday Lamb and the Slow Cooker Beef Brisket, as well as lots of other dishes.

Serves 4

1 cauliflower, broken into florets

spray oil

garlic powder, to taste

salt and ground black pepper

Preheat the oven to 220°C (200°C fan oven), Gas 7. Spread the cauliflower florets over a baking tray. Spray with the oil and season well with salt and pepper and the garlic powder. Bake for 20–30 minutes or until golden.

EASY GREMOLATA

If you are looking for a little something to elevate your fish dishes, this is a really easy way to brighten them up. I serve this with roasted cod and sweet potato wedges. You can also swirl it into soups and stews, add it to pasta or serve it with eggs or meat.

Serves 4

zest and juice of 2 lemons

1 bunch of fresh parsley, leaves only

2 large garlic cloves, peeled and left whole

sea salt

Put the lemon zest, parsley and garlic into a small food processor (I use a NutriBullet) and add some salt. Squeeze in the lemon juice, then whizz it all up until it is chopped and combined. Done!

CRANBERRY GRAVY

One of the best things for me about going to Ikea is eating the meatballs and the lovely loganberry sauce that goes with them. This is my take on that. This cranberry gravy goes well with meats, and sausages and mash to make them into something a little more special. You don't need a lot of this, as it is super-sweet. I guarantee the kids will love it.

Serves 4

500g cranberry sauce

50ml soy sauce

100ml orange juice

Combine all the ingredients together in a small saucepan and heat over a medium-low heat until piping hot.

PART 5

Christmas – Be Prepared!

17

The Organised Christmas Countdown

How could I not include a section about Christmas in this book? I love Christmas! When I first shared my Organised Christmas plan with TeamTOMM, everyone went crazy for it, and I was inundated with messages from people who were having their most relaxing Christmas ever. People were actually enjoying the festivities rather than just orchestrating them. Just like with TOMM, it was an absolute joy to see how something that I had been following privately for years was helping other people make the most of their time with their families in December. After all isn't that what Christmas is all about?

Christmas is hands down my favourite time of the year. When I was growing up, my mum and dad would close their fish and chip shop for two weeks and that meant we could all spend some rare and lovely quality time together. My mum was always a massive Christmas fan and has always loved Christmas to be an over-the-top affair – think mad glitter and lots of lights. To this day she still sends Christmas cards with a glitter bomb in the envelope. My mum being a Christmas fan made it such a magical experience for me as a child and when I became a mum I was excited to recreate the same sort of magic.

I have such wonderful memories of Decembers gone by. I hope that when my own children remember their child-hood they too will be filled with joy when they look back at Christmases past.

REALITY – MY FIRST CHRISTMAS AS A MUM

We all know that very often the romantic visions that dance in our heads of the way we want things to be are not always how they turn out, and this was the case for my first ever Christmas as a mum. Just as I was sold the perfect-mum life image, I also fell hook, line and sinker for the Christmas-card ideal of how I thought Christmas should be. Sadly, all that happened that first year was that I was left disillusioned and not at all merry. I had worn myself out trying to make everything perfect, and we all know how that ends up.

Do you watch Christmas adverts or retro Mariah Carey and Wham videos and wonder why your Christmas isn't full of white mohair roll necks, perfectly fitting jeans, snow and expertly wrapped presents under an enviably decorated tree in an Alpine lodge? I think we all do. The reality is that most of us are sitting eating our turkey around a table on mismatched chairs, and yet we still manage to have a fabulous time. A perfect Christmas is a fool's errand. When you learn to let go, you can soon get all the magic back, and then some.

It is true that Christmas takes preparation and attention to detail (and money). And it is also true that just like there is no housework fairy, there is no Christmas fairy either. The magic has to come from you, and this isn't as easy as it sounds.

Tom was six months old when we had our first Christmas together, and I have such a vivid memory of sitting by the tree on Christmas Eve having just finished frantically wrapping the presents. I felt stressed and worn out. The Baileys that I had been sipping while wrapping didn't taste as good as I had imagined it would and the reality was that in about five hours' time Tom would be awake, and I would start Christmas Day exhausted and not feeling very festive.

Prior to becoming a mum, Christmas wasn't such a big deal to prepare for. I only had to buy presents for a couple of people (so the budget wasn't stretched) and I went round to my mum and dad's and watched them cook the turkey. Pre-kids, Christmas was something that was enjoyed and something that happened to me. I could look forward to Christmas lunch and passively partake in it. But when you are in charge of a child's happiness at Christmas it brings a whole other dimension to the Most Wonderful Time of the Year, and the pressure can be overwhelming. Add this to the normal day-to-day running of the family home, keeping on budget, holding down a job and maintaining a relationship, and you are left with a festive pressure cooker.

On my very first Christmas as a mum I fell into the trap that most parents do every single day of the year: I put myself last. And this meant that my usual enjoyment of Christmas wasn't there because it was replaced by lists of jobs that I had to do. My days were filled with doing things that I had never done before, like booking Father Christmas tickets and trying to work out when to fit in Christmas lunch with a six-month-old who would need a day-time nap.

ENTER THE ORGANISED CHRISTMAS

There is nothing quite like the baptism of fire that is cooking Christmas dinner for the first time. All this made me feel a bit flat, because as much as it was amazing to see Christmas through the eyes of my baby, it felt that the magic had gone because it was now up to me to orchestrate that magic for someone else – a sure-fire way to kill the illusion.

After all the wrapping paper had been tidied away and the last of the mince pies had been devoured, I made a promise to myself that next year was going to be different, and the Organised Christmas Countdown was born. Much like TOMM itself, the Organised Christmas Countdown was created from my own frustrations and needs and, just like TOMM, it has changed the way that thousands of people do Christmas for the better. Let me tell you my secrets. (PS: this part of the book is not for Father Christmas believers, so make sure you keep it out of sight. Let's keep that magic alive.)

THE 13-WEEK CHRISTMAS COUNTDOWN

The next sentence might shock you, especially if you are one of those people who doesn't start thinking about Christmas until the first door of the advent calendar is opened. I start planning for Christmas in early September – exactly 13 weeks before 1 December. Each year I sit down at my calendar and mark in my diary the Monday that is 13 weeks before 1 December.

Before you run off in horror, let me explain why I do this. I want to enjoy December, and I want you all to enjoy December, too. I want to be able to sit in the audience at my kids' carol concert and be fully present, not with half my thoughts trying to work out if I have enough in the budget to buy panto tickets, only to have a furtive glance at my phone to see that the tickets all sold out weeks ago. I want to feel happy and full of excitement when I hear The Pogues belt out their tune for the first time, without it putting the fear of God into me that I am in no way ready.

With that in mind, I start early, so that I can tick a couple of jobs off my list each week, meaning that, slowly but surely, Christmas will all be sorted by the time 1 December rolls around. And it *will* roll around, sooner than you think. You all know by now that my philosophy of little and often works. And it works because it stops things from becoming overwhelming and a massive list of jobs forming. Little and often is the way that the Organised Christmas Countdown is structured too. By following along, you will free up your time in December to have fun and make some real memories with your friends and family. Once you have done one Organised Christmas you won't look back; it will change the way you do Christmas forever.

LET'S GET FESTIVE!

Sit down and work out when week 1 needs to start. This will be exactly 13 weeks from 1 December. I always like to start it on a Monday.

Week 1

If you have young children in primary school, try to find out when the Nativity or any other Christmas events are happening. This way anyone who wants to come along can make sure they book the time off work well in advance. This is particularly important for people who work shifts or work in an occupation where leave has to be scheduled well ahead of time. If dates aren't released yet, make a note in your diary to check in a couple of weeks.

Start thinking about food. I have an online delivery saver with my supermarket. This gives me a priority Christmas delivery slot, which plays a big part in cutting down the stresstive part of Christmas for me. I don't want to be roaming the aisles fighting for my turkey or sprout tree; I want to be drinking mulled wine while the very nice people deliver it all to my door. If you feel the same about supermarkets in December, sign up this week. Check the small print and see if your supermarket gives you a priority slot. In years gone by I would set my alarm for 4am and head to a 24-hour supermarket to get my Christmas food shopping done. I did this because I wanted to do it in as calm an environment as possible (one year, I kid you not, I saw someone doing their Christmas shopping in their slippers and dressing gown). But now I order online and it is much more civilised and much less frantic. You can't get much calmer than ordering your Christmas food from your sofa in your PJs.

Another important thing to remember is that if you are venturing into your supermarket super-early to get your Christmas food, the alcohol aisle might not be open due to licensing laws – been there, done that.

Book your tickets to see The Big Dude in the red suit. The popular events sell out fast. If the event you want hasn't got tickets on sale yet, find out when they are due to be released and get it in the diary.

If you want to do more Christmassy events this year, research them and book them in the diary. This will help you to spread the cost, and you will make sure that you won't miss out on tickets for the popular events. Do you always say you'll go to a pantomime or go ice skating, but you never get round to it? This is your year.

Week 2

Now is the perfect time to have a toy and clothes clear-out. Do it now before everything starts to get crazy busy. Your kids will be back at school and the chances are that you will have accumulated some junk piles over the summer holidays. Now is the time to battle the clutter (don't forget about the

Clutter Buster section on page 26 if you need some extra motivation). Let's face it, there will be an influx of new stuff coming your way soon. Get ruthless: either donate, bin or list anything on selling sites that is no longer wanted (this way you can rake in some extra cash for present-buying).

If you know that you will be travelling to see family or friends via train this year, book your tickets as early as you can, and if you need to book hotel rooms, do that now, too. They will be so much cheaper and there will be better availability.

If you are spending time away from home, make sure you have planned for your pets, and book the kennels or cat sitters now. They get booked up quickly, so you don't want to be left in a spot with no one to look after Rover and Tiddles.

If you want to plan a festive get-together with friends, pick the date this week and send out save-the-date messages to everyone. People get booked up fast at this time of the year (there are only so many weekends in December). Get in there early to make sure that people can make it. If you need babysitters, make sure you get them booked in too this week.

Week 3

Have a freezer clear-out this week. Is there a lonely box of frozen mince pies lurking from Christmas last year? Get rid of any suspicious-looking packages that are no longer labelled, and try to use up as much food as you can, so that you don't waste anything. Any money that you save on your food bill while you are eating up the contents of your freezer can be put towards your Christmas budget. If necessary, give your freezer a defrost. An empty freezer will give the bakers among us the chance to fill them up with lots of festive treats.

If you normally buy your advent calendar from the super-market in a panic on 30 November, now is your chance to get one step ahead of the game and treat yourself to something a little special. There are loads of amazing advent calendars around now, from beauty ones to Lego ones, but they usually go on sale quite early, and the best ones always sell out fast. Have a little scout around this week and see if there are any that tickle your fancy.

Week 4

The main task for this week is to set your budget. Think about everything: food, gifts and travel costs, but also remember to plan for all the little miscellaneous things that can add up to quite a hefty sum (such as additional petrol bills, wrapping paper, cards, stamps and batteries). Your budget can be as detailed as you like, but the most important thing is that it must be realistic. The best way to do this is to work out how many pay days you have between now and The Big Day, and plan how much money you can set aside between now and then for the festivities.

The other golden rule is not to overstretch yourself or you will be in for a miserable start to the new year. January is bad enough as it is without having to go through the whole month skint.

Make a list of who you will be buying presents for, and set a maximum budget for each person. Once you have made your budget and you are happy with it, make a commitment to yourself to stick to it. Over the remaining weeks in the Christmas Countdown buy presents when you have the funds, and wrap them as you go. Remember that your aim is to have it all wrapped up (pun intended) by 1 December.

Week 5

This week's job is to go through all your Christmas decorations and do a stock check. Remember that the sole purpose of this plan is to make sure that you enjoy Christmas, and one of the best bits is getting into the festive spirit by decorating your tree. That romantic image that we all have of Christmas will not be how it goes if your lights don't work or all your baubles are smashed. Be your future friend and check it all now, even if you have to go into the dizzy heights of the loft.

Week 6

Are you planning to go out this New Year's Eve? If the answer to that is yes, then you need to get it booked in now and also get your babysitter booked in too. If you usually spend New Year's Eve with a major fear of missing out, this is your year to make sure that it doesn't happen again.

Week 7

If you have not started to get serious about present-buying, now is the time. This is especially important if you have a partner (or other family member) who is seriously hard to buy for. You need to talk to them now about what they want. You don't want to have a last-minute scramble, panic buying them a present, because this will totally ruin your festive flow.

Speak to the kids and let them know that Father Christmas and his elves have a cut-off date for list amendments. This way you won't be in the awful situation where you've spent all your budget and they then think of something that they really want, which means you have to overload your credit card.

Week 8

Take time to book in all your appointments this week: hair, eyebrows, nails, and so on. There is nothing worse than phoning up to get yourself looking hot to trot and finding that everything is booked up.

Do you have pets that need taking care of? Make sure you stock up on their regular flea treatment and also get them booked in at the groomers.

Put some thought into whether you want to start any new traditions. Now that you are organised, and everything is under control, you might have more energy and headspace to add some extra-special trimmings to your family's festive fun. If you want to do elf-on-the-shelf, start thinking of stuff you can do now with the mischievous imp. Don't do what I did the first year ours arrived and panicked every night at 10pm because I had no idea what to do.

Book your Christmas and New Year's Eve taxis.

Week 9

If you send Christmas cards, buy them and write them this week, write the envelopes and put them somewhere safe ready to post on 1 December. If your children are at school and like to send cards to their classmates, buy these this week and get them to write a handful every now and again. This will stop the kind of mammoth card-writing session where the handwriting ends up extremely questionable by card number 21 of 30.

Make sure to continue to wrap your presents as you go – and also to make sure that all presents are clearly labelled (or you will forget who they are for). If you are posting abroad, check the last postal dates now and plan what you are going to send and when it needs to be sent by.

Week 10

'Tis the time to think about your Christmas food (again). How you approach your Christmas menu will depend on your own individual preferences. I personally mark Christmas Eve, Christmas Day and Boxing Day as special eating days. This means that we get extra treats and posher grub than normal. By marking your special food days, it will stop you over-ordering, and it also stops me from overeating into the New Year. Sit down and plan your food, and make sure you keep to budget. I think it is really important to keep it all in perspective and not to let the costs spiral out of control. It is so easy to get caught up in all the marketing hype at Christmas, especially when the glitzy adverts start appearing on the television. Remember: Christmas dinner is just a Sunday lunch with a few bells and whistles.

GEM'S TOP TIP

 If you are ordering a turkey, make sure it fits into your oven. If you are buying a frozen turkey, work out how long it will take to defrost, then mark this on your calendar or set a reminder on your phone.

Week 11

It is time for the pre-Christmas spruce-up and home check. It is always best to start with a clean slate before the decorations go up. If you follow along with TOMM, this week will be a walk in the park for you. But there are a couple of extra things that I want you to look out for. If you are new to TOMM, this week will see you giving your home a reboot, and for that I suggest using the Messy House Boot Camp.

While you are doing your pre-Christmas home check, here are some handy things for you to have on your radar.

- Make sure you have enough tree light bulbs. Since most fairy lights are now LED, it can be hard to get replacement bulbs, so make sure you test yours. And remember, it's always handy to have some spare (just in case!).
- Have a decent stockpile of batteries, because there is always that one toy.
- Test your smoke alarms.
- Finally, check through your medicine cabinet, throw out anything that is past its best and restock as necessary. Now is the time to also think about any regular medication that you or your family members take and make sure that you put it in your diary to get any repeat prescriptions in plenty of time.

Week 12

If you are having guests for Christmas, make sure you have enough chairs/glasses/crockery and cutlery (you can hire more if necessary).

Buy your Christmas crackers.

Buy two or three emergency gifts. Good ones to go for are generic bottles of wine for the grown-ups and gift cards for the kiddies. This will have you covered just in case you find yourself in that awkward situation where someone surprises you with a gift and you haven't bought them one.

Think about teacher gifts this week, and get them bought and wrapped.

Week 13

It is time to decorate. This is the final week of the plan, and this is the best bit. I always decorate my house on the first weekend of December, so that is all there is left to do. Go as crazy or as minimal as you want. Remember: this is your Christmas – there are no rules. Once you have put the decorations up, it's time for some final checks:

- Do you have a corkscrew?
- If you are entertaining, do you have enough soft drinks for the drivers? How about making them a lovely driver's punch?
- Do you have enough foil to use for resting the meat?
- Go back over the Christmas Countdown and make sure that you have ticked everything off.

Have a wonderful Christmas; you have worked so hard all year and you deserve to enjoy the season and all the wonders it brings. But a word to the wise: because you are prepped so well in advance you need to guard yourself against the Christmas Twitch – it's a bit like The Grinch but The Twitch preys on your weakness to overspend. Don't give in and start buying extra little bits here and there, because you might blow your budget. Stand firm and enjoy the ride.

Have a good one!

18

Christmas Survival Tips for First-Time Hosters

Have you taken up the mantle of hosting Christmas dinner for the first time this year? Did it seem like a really good idea when you offered to take the strain at the family barbecue way back in August? Christmas dinner can strike the fear of God into the most confident of cooks. And the reason? The responsibility – the slow creep of Christmas pressure that makes your blood run a little bit colder, because once again the enjoyment of others lies in your hands.

Fear not; as always, I'm here to help. The most important thing to remember about Christmas dinner is that it has been made out to be a mythical beast, and it has a bit of an over-inflated ego. If all the hype were to be believed, you would be forgiven for thinking that it should come with a health warning for being the most stressful meal you will ever make. This isn't true. There is an awful lot of hand wringing going on over those Brussels sprouts, and most of us don't even like them.

The trick is not to give in to the self-doubt and to boss your own Christmas dinner (however you do it). This chapter is all how about to maintain a level head when everyone around you is losing theirs. If this is your first time hosting, then let me guide you through the madness.

If you don't normally cook throughout the year, you are not going to suddenly turn into Nigella or Delia at the stroke of midnight on 24 December. You need to be realistic and work to your skills. Remember: the whole philosophy that I have going on about with the Organised Christmas? That's right: you need to enjoy it, too. You won't enjoy it if you are stressing about whether your bread sauce tastes like bread sauce, because having never eaten it before you have no idea what it actually tastes like.

Christmas dinner is basically a fancy Sunday roast, so don't let it get you in a tizz. Furthermore, it is your Christmas dinner, which means that you get to make the rules. Don't fall into the trap of cooking Brussels sprouts because you think you need to – if you don't like sprouts, don't cook them. The same applies to your meat of choice. In my experience fewer people than you think actually enjoy turkey. How often do you see turkey on the menu at other times of the year? If you want chicken, have chicken, and if you want beef, have beef. Here are my top tips to help you hold it all together if you are hosting Christmas dinner for the first time.

THE FOOD

The main thing that you need to do is to keep your meal plan really simple. If you are not confident about having lots of things cooking at the same time, go with quality over quantity. It is much better for you to have a few dishes done really well than lots of things that are a bit lacklustre.

Don't feel the pressure to have a starter; there will be enough food coming your guests' way.

Try not to have too many side dishes and festive trimmings. Not only will it create extra effort for you, but you will also be heartbroken when no one eats everything. You will find yourself forcing down one extra mouthful of sprouts with pancetta because you have worked really hard on creating a feast. It will be far better for you, and on everyone else's digestive systems, if you pick your two favourite vegetable side dishes and put everything you have into them.

Don't feel under pressure to make all your condiments – even I don't do this. I always buy the cranberry sauce and apple sauce. And if you want to buy your gravy ready-made, do so. All you need to do on the day is decant them into posh serving dishes (if you want to) and you are good to go.

As mentioned earlier, make sure your turkey fits into the oven. This is really crucial, as you can't have your dinner falling at the first hurdle because you haven't been able to cook it. If there are not that many of you, perhaps consider buying a turkey crown instead, it will save you money and make sure that there is as little food waste as possible.

This next part is not one for the traditionalists If you are not a great cook, and you are panicking at the thought of hosting, then stop stressing. There is no medal at the end of all this. Remember: the aim of the game is for you to have fun, too. If you really can't handle cooking things from scratch, it is totally acceptable to buy ready-made. The most effort will be in opening the packets and popping them in the oven at the right temperature. Some supermarkets have caught on to this and have Christmas food that all cooks at the same temperature, meaning that you have to do as little thinking as possible. Sherry anyone? And remember that if the packets don't give a fan oven temperature and you are using a fan oven, you will need to deduct 20°C from the stated temperature. All the recipes in this book give regular and fan oven temperatures.

DON'T GET FLUMMOXED

Try to stay as relaxed as possible I know this might be easier said than done, but if you are in a flap, your guests will pick up on your anxiety. If your voice is shrill and your face is as red as a Father Christmas's suit, then it will set the scene for a tense atmosphere, and I am hazarding a guess that this is not the ambiance that you will be going for. If it is all getting a bit too much, head upstairs or outside for a few minutes and take some deep breaths. Better still, confide in someone who is close to you and tell them that you are feeling nervous and ask them to be your wingman. There is strength in numbers.

If it is the timings that are worrying you, then work backwards. Tell people a rough time that you are going to eat. Don't commit to a definite time or you will put yourself under additional and unnecessary pressure. Work out how long everything will take to cook and what time you will need to start cooking it, write it all down (not forgetting to factor in time for letting the meat rest) and it will stop the overwhelming feeling from taking over.

Make sure you have enough oven space for everything that you plan to cook. Make use of your microwave if you need to, and if you can, try to prepare some components in advance.

Try to make sure that you do your all your prep work before the guests arrive. Don't forget that they are here to see you, and this means that they will want to talk to you. This can put you under pressure if everyone gathers in the kitchen while you are trying to do your thing. Keep calm and peel your potatoes and vegetables, and put them in cold water until you are ready to cook them.

If you are not used to serving up, ask someone else to carve the meat – they will be flattered that you have asked them.

Make someone else drinks monitor and task them with making sure that glasses are charged.

Put as much food as you can on the table so that people can help themselves. This way you won't be stuck in the kitchen serving up the last few plates while half the guests are waiting with their food going cold.

Serve your food onto warm plates (not hot or people might burn themselves). A great way to do this is to have your plates in a sink of hot, clean water before you serve your food. Try not to serve onto cold plates, as this will mean the food goes cold quicker.

Wear something that is comfortable and that you are not going to overheat in. You will be cooking, and this means that you will get hot, so keep this in mind and avoid wearing a thick jumper or you will end up with a face as flushed as Santa's.

THE TABLE

Make sure that you have enough chairs for everyone.

Set the table the night before so that you can really make sure you have it looking just as you want it. By being your future friend and doing it when you have plenty of time you can really go to town.

Make sure that you are sitting in a spot where you can exit quickly and get into the kitchen. Don't put yourself in a corner, otherwise you will have to squeeze past Auntie Edna to get to the oven.

If you are having a centrepiece, keep it low so that you can see everyone at the table. A massive vase of flowers in people's eye line is going to hamper conversation somewhat (but perhaps that wouldn't be a bad thing where some guests are concerned).

Keep place settings as simple as possible, people are going to want to be able to move their elbows and also be able to reach for sauces. They will also need the ability to freely pass down the extra roasties, so try to keep as much space as you can.

BE MORE FESTIVE AND LESS STRESSTIVE

Christmas can be as complicated and fancy as we make it, so please don't feel the need to put yourself under any additional pressure. When I started planning and prepping for that first Christmas I will hold my hands up and say that I overdid it a little bit and I was my own worst enemy. Over the years I have found ways to simplify the prep and make sure that I am not a frazzled bundle of nerves by Christmas Eve.

It is so important to keep it all in perspective. There is no such thing as the perfect Christmas and, just like trying to get the perfect show home, trying to recreate a picture-postcard Christmas will break you. If you expect too much of the festive period, you might end up being disappointed. Remember: life likes to throw in the odd curveball (like your oven element going just as you are about to pop in the roasties), so it is much better to approach this time of year with a relaxed attitude and you (and everyone else around you) will be much happier for it because you have not turned into Christmaszilla. With that in mind, here are my top ways of keeping the blood pressure as low as possible throughout December.

Don't overload your diary in December. As much as it is nice to see family and friends, keep in mind that there are still only so many hours in the day and only 31 days in December. Be realistic with your diary and don't be afraid to book a few get-togethers in January. Things are always a bit boring then anyway, so it will be nice to have something to look forward to.

When it is time to open the presents on Christmas Day, make sure that you have a big box ready to collect all the wrapping paper. That way you won't be surrounded by a sea of paper and ribbon.

If you have young children who have toys that will need setting up, consider doing this on Christmas Eve after they have gone to bed. You can still make it look magical with bows and ribbons, but it will stop their frustration levels and impatience from boiling over while you are trying to set it up. It is not relaxing at six o'clock on Christmas morning when you have a small child hopping from one foot to the other because you are not setting up their train track fast enough. Setting up in advance means that your Christmas morning will be spent sitting watching them playing rather than hunting for one of those tiny screwdrivers that all toy packaging seems to need these days.

Set up all your favourite Christmas programmes ready to record. This way, if you have any guests in the house and there is a clash of what people want to watch, it will be fine because you can always watch yours at leisure when they have gone home. And you will probably enjoy it more because you can put on your PJs.

Try to get out for walks in the fresh air. This is crucial, as it will help with your mental clarity and also give you much needed headspace. Don't be afraid to take some me time and go for a walk on your own. Christmas is a busy time filled with noise and lots of people, so make sure that you take the time to reset.

If you are worried about money, make sure that you manage people's expectations, including the kids. Never put yourself into debt trying to keep up with what you think is expected of you at Christmas. Turn off the Christmas adverts if you need to and explain to the kids that you are trying to stay within a budget. It is much better to buy one or two much-wanted presents than lots of bits that will never get played with again.

If you are worried that the present piles won't be big enough, try this: go and ask your kids to write down what they got for Christmas last year. I bet they won't be able to remember half of it, so try not to overthink it.

Conclusion

You are now a fully fledged member of TeamTOMM. I truly hope that you have found my advice both helpful and inspiring. If you find yourself with a renewed vigour to take control of the housework, make sure to check out the TeamTOMM Facebook group. It is a treasure trove of support, hints and tips, and it should be your first port of call for any cleaning conundrums.

If you want further motivation and are keen to see how I fit TOMM into my day, you can find me over on Instagram, and I would love it if you tagged me into your social media posts or dropped me an email; it makes me so happy to see how TOMM is helping people.

Now go forth and regain control of your house, and remember:

DO YOUR 30 MINUTES, BE YOUR FUTURE FRIEND AND, MOST IMPORTANTLY, ENJOY YOUR HOUSEWORK-FREE WEEKENDS.

Wishing you all the luck in the world,
Gem

Index

(Page numbers in **bold** refer to recipes)